AWARE OF *Utopia*

AWARE OF *Utopia*

Edited by
DAVID W. PLATH

UNIVERSITY OF ILLINOIS PRESS
Urbana Chicago London

© *1971 by The Board of Trustees of the University of Illinois*
Manufactured in the United States of America
Library of Congress Catalog Card No. 73–146010

252 00168 0

CONTENTS

What if there is not another bright spot in the wide world, and what if this is a very small one? Turn your eye toward it when you are tired of looking into chaos, and you will catch a glimpse of a better world.

JOHN HUMPHREY NOYES

 FOREWORD

Scorn is still the standard attitude toward utopia. The good liberal continues to echo the spirit that Macaulay once expressed when he said he would much rather have "an acre in Middlesex than a principality in Utopia." The good Marxian continues to accept Engels's verdict that utopian socialism is "unscientific" and a shameful heresy. And even a dissenting Marxist like Milovan Djilas equates utopia with dogmatism and tyranny, and opts instead for an "unperfect" society.[1]

But utopia—that perennial place of impossible dreams—endures despite generations of utopicide. The utopian underground is coming to the surface today in many guises. The Now Generation embarks upon communal efforts to subtract materialism from industrial technology (one report claims that there

[1] Milovan Djilas, *The Unperfect Society: Beyond the New Class* (New York: Harcourt, Brace and World, 1969), esp. pp. 4–5.

are as many as 500 such communities in the United States).[2] The developing nations pursue models of modernity that hold out a promise of affluence without alienation. Futurology has become a serious field of study; assemblies gather to preview the year 2000.[3] And even the president of the American Sociological Association addresses his reality-minded colleagues on "The Utility of Utopias."[4]

So utopia has not become just a petrified pun. Men continue to envision—and strive to build—a more harmonious society, a society hypothetically placed in a land not found in the *National Geographic* atlas but which determined travelers can reach. These images of a beautiful nowhere transcend the present, for they do not merely extrapolate current trends or posit a minor shuffling of priorities. They start from a counter-stance to the present and reach out for radically different principles and patterns of human action.

Like all men, the utopian artist must draw upon the idioms of his time and site, and wrestle with the restraints of his local milieu. But he aspires to rise above them. As Seiji Nuita puts it (in the essay which follows), the utopian leaps over social barriers in order to attack them, so to speak, from the other side. Indeed, the utopian yearns not just for local improvements; he reaches out for the universal, for a culture more cleansed of pain, waste, and inhumanity than any yet devised on this planet.

Because of his ambition, others often accuse him of playing Moses, of supposing he has already stood atop Sinai and seen the promised land. But ordinarily he does not claim such perfect vision; he asks only that we suspend disbelief in the possibility of a radical leap out of the ruts of human history. He may not

[2] "Year of the Commune," *Newsweek*, August 18, 1969, pp. 89–90.
[3] Daniel Bell et al., *Toward the Year 2000: Work in Progress*. Special issue of *Daedalus* 96, No. 3 (1967).
[4] Wilbert E. Moore, "The Utility of Utopias," *American Sociological Review* 31 (1966):765–72.

have a blueprint in his pocket, but his certainty that utopia is visible, even in soft focus, can unleash in him great floods of creative energy. Aldous Huxley points this up nicely in *Island*. In this novel, a Scottish doctor has teamed up with the local raja to transform the backward and out-of-the-way island of Pala. "Make it over into what?" asks a visiting journalist. The physician's son replies:

That was a question he couldn't have answered. In those early days he had no plan—only a set of likes and dislikes. There were things about Pala that he liked, and plenty of others that he didn't like at all. Things about Europe that he detested, and things he passionately approved of. Things he had seen on his travels that seemed to make good sense, and things that filled him with disgust. People, he was beginning to understand, are at once the beneficiaries and the victims of their culture. It brings them to flower; but it also nips them in the bud or plants a canker at the heart of the blossom. Might it not be possible, on this forbidden island, to avoid the cankers, minimize the nippings, and make the individual blooms more beautiful? That was the question to which, implicitly at first, then with a growing awareness of what they were really up to, Dr. Andrew and the Raja were trying to find an answer.

. . . It was an enormous ambition, an ambition totally impossible of fulfillment; but at least it had the merit of spurring them on, of making them rush in where angels feared to tread—with results that sometimes proved, to everyone's astonishment, that they had not been quite such fools as they looked.[5]

Is this kind of yearning and striving for an "ideal place" a habit peculiar to the West? Scholars often define the utopian imagination in terms of the set of form elements found in More's *Utopia* and its many imitators. Utopia in this formal sense is a sketch of a harmonious society, outside the known world but

[5] Aldous Huxley, *Island* (New York: Bantam Books, 1963), pp. 129–30.

peopled with real and ordinary (albeit much improved) humans, as reported to us by travelers or native informants. Men do seem to have hit upon this particular combination only rarely outside the West, but the elements of it can be found widely elsewhere in other formats. Men everywhere seem addicted to visions of ideal otherness, although often enough it can only be achieved by death-and-transfiguration, or is the gift of infra-human mammals or supra-human spaceniks. So if one is willing to widen the definition to include other types of transcendent social vision, one can begin to see many varieties of utopian image-work in mankind's many traditions. Some rough-and-ready surveying has been done along these lines, but it tends to suffer from Western bias and from the difficulties any man has at commanding a knowledge of more than a handful of other cultures.

Further, and more exacting, studies of the form elements of utopian imagery will be worthy in their own right. They can add a new domain to the structuralist approach being used these days with such Levi-Straussian gusto to decompose analytically all sorts of products of the human imagination. However, the authors in this volume take a different tack. They are less interested in utopia's literary forms than in its social functions. They see it less as a combination of motifs, more as a cluster of motives. Each in his own way, they are seeking to understand how, in human affairs—to borrow a phrase from Karl Mannheim—the impossible gives birth to the possible. What, they are asking, is the "utility" of holding an image of a transcendent-yet-real, and realizable, world?

Taking a cue from Max Weber's studies of the great religions, we might pose the problem in this way: What circumstances inspire men to choose utopian rather than other conceivable forms of world rejection? And what action consequences follow when men are taken up in the grip of a utopian preview?

In contrast to, say, the hermit or the migrant, the utopian rejects his world by seeking to transform it. His rejection is wedded to a demand for domestic action, for he does not believe —like the chiliast—that a new life will transpire by divine machination or by the working out of automatic dialectics of history. Paradoxically, then, he is called to become a politician by the very act in which he professes to be above ordinary politics.

He may wish to remake all mankind, but as a practical activist he is likely to decide to concentrate upon one or another human unit as his agency for change. He may favor a class of persons, as does the Marxist or Maoist in his vision of uniting workers or peasants of the world. He may favor a region, as did proponents of the Greater East Asia Co-Prosperity Sphere. He may favor his own nation, as do modernizing elites on several continents. He may favor operating upon social relationships, as did Japan's Nishida Tenkō with his vision of the transmuting power of selfless service. Or he may, of course, favor building a pilot-plant little community—as with Fourier, or Robert Owen, or *Walden Two*—where he will test and at the same time demonstrate the values of his new life.

The term "utopian" ordinarily has been applied only to the last of these. But similar couplings—of world rejection with practical struggle to build a grand new world—also motivate various other kinds of cultural activism. By uncovering this utopian element, one can win fresh insight into an array of social movements that might otherwise seem bizarre. One also wins fresh appreciation for the power of positive utopian thinking. This sense of discovery—of the payoff that comes from seeking out the utopian elements in human behavior—threads through this collection and shows up especially in the essays by George B. Bikle, Jr., and Harold Gould.

Scholarship is a reflexive as well as reflective act, the more so the more it touches human concerns. The object of study sheds light back upon the subjective life-situation of the student. Renewed interest on the part of the social scientist in the study of utopian motives is in fair degree, I suspect, linked to renewed hopes that he will engage in utopian thinking for the benefit of his fellow men. To be sure, many of his practical clients want of him no more than accurate information about recent mass attitudes, or reliable projections of recent trends. But increasingly, in our end-of-ideology, God-is-dead atmosphere, the social scientist finds a secular congregation calling upon him for a transcending vision.

This "clerisy" role has never been absent from the practice of social science, but it has been masked and muted by a generation of practicioners idolatrous of fact. Now the role daily grows more public. Investigations are expected to be not only reliable but relevant. And one of our most relevant needs is for previews of a "post-modern" utopia that can both inspire and guide action in a world gone sour with the ethics of overkill. The social scientist is being asked not only to examine the worlds in which men do or have in fact lived, but also to scrutinize with equal rigor the worlds in which men might come, in fact, to be. Margaret Mead's suggestion, made some years ago, was that we build a social planetarium, where people could go to contemplate projections of alternative future cultural constellations.

Utopianism might also be able to furnish the moral foundation that is missing from much social science practice today. Nuita suggests this in his essay; Robert Nisbet, among others, has written in a similar vein:

> At first thought, utopianism and a genuine social science may seem to be incompatible. But they are not. Utopianism is compatible with everything but determinism, and it can as easily be the over-all context of social science as can any other creative vision.

. . . Utopianism, after all, is social planning, and planning is indispensable in the kind of world that technology, democracy, and high population bring.[6]

In this book, James A. Dator's essay confronts these questions as they bear upon the future of politics. The rest of our authors are more conventional in their scholarship, directing their wit and energy to the making of concepts and typologies and to be ing accurate as well as original as they explore the varieties utopian motives and the parts they play in the lives of other But all of us hope that these chapters will aid and en others who are struggling to make nowhere be some

These essays derive from a Conference on Uto parative Focus, held on the Urbana campus of the Illinois, May 9–10, 1968. The University's C national Comparative Studies sponsored and ference; the Illini Union provided rooms Many persons helped, but I want to gi Center's chairman, Professor Joseph suggested the conference and who it. Participants included—in addi of these essays—Arthur Best Seattle), Robert Boguslaw (' Maren Lockwood (Bostor versity), and Stuart Um

Conference session avoid the ritualized sterile—and dowr another topic r and notes to Thus we c

[6] Robe versity Pres

work we were pursuing and to clarify our ideas by trying to communicate them to others.

Some of this work already has been published elsewhere; some of it eventually will be. In this respect, this collection of essays offers a skewed sampling of the problems we took up in our sessions. This is particularly true as regards the utopian element in social science—we devoted a long and full session to it —represented here only by Dator's essay. In this foreword and the introductions to the main sections of the book, I have incorporated a number of ideas which came out during the conference and which may not be obvious from the essays themselves.

I have standardized matters of style and referencing in these essays; aside from that I have edited lightly. I have preferred to let each author develop freely his own line of approach, even though as often as not I disagree with it. This may annoy the kind of reader who wants a battery of authors kept in firm check and made to maneuver like a close-order drill team. Some-ay there will, I hope, be coordinate research on utopia. But co-linate research requires long-term cohabitation and massive s of money. We had funds enough for a fruitful conference, ur budget was rather less than that of the National Aero-s and Space Administration. NASA has been able to land the moon; perhaps, given equal backing, we might be and men in utopia. Many people believe it can be done, f is incipient action.

DAVID W. PLATH

of Illinois, Urbana

P A

The Utopi

INTRODUCTION

If we assume that the utopian imaginatio
West, we confront the problem of pinpo
where. This was the main reason for d
one on utopia in *comparative* focus.
Daedalus symposium of 1965 ha
utopian tradition.[1] We hoped
we could suggest some frui
cultural inquiry into the r
array of such image-wo
these texts to the kind
inspire their creati
utopian against d
in similar circ

[1] *Daedal*
version w
Frank E. Ma.

Frank Manuel's essay in the *Daedalus* symposium offers one interesting point of departure.[2] Manuel posits three epochs in the Western utopian tradition, each with a characteristic manner of localizing its vision of the transcendent better world.

Eutopia typified the sixteenth through eighteenth centuries, More's book being the type-case. The urge to stand outside their own society propelled men to a contemporary but distant space; eutopia was a bright little island somewhere beyond the sea.

Euchronia was the nineteenth-century mode. The better world was "here" instead of "there," but located in a beautiful time to come. Bellamy's *Looking Backward* is the type-case, his Bostonians of the future contemplating with developed-nation smugness the underdeveloped Boston of archaic 1880.

Eupsychia is our present fashion. The better world is neither "there" nor "here," it is quite simply within us—to use the hippie term, "a vision of beautiful people." Skinner's *Walden Two* can erve as a type-specimen: it may be atypical in its fondness for dgets and behavioral engineering, but it portrays a "non-repres- e" culture where work is play and all life is libidinized.

he typology can be used to uncover affinities between a utopian of projection and the life-context which sustained it. Manuel o in a number of interesting ways; let me merely illustrate. s More's epoch, for example, was also the time of Europe's ry" of the rest of mankind. The notion of an ideal island e" very likely was believable to a degree that would be us to expect of a generation that takes Telstar for en Huxley's twentieth-century *Island* is well within trated by journalist-spies and eventually conquered by nation lusting for resources.

rye offers a well-turned contrast between eutopia eupsychia which would be believable today:

chological History of Utopias," ibid., pp. 293–322.

The great classical utopias derived their form from city-states and, though imaginary, were thought of as being, like the city-states, exactly locatable in space. Modern utopias derive their form from a uniform pattern of civilization spread over the whole globe, and so are thought of as world-states, taking up all the available space. It is clear that if there is to be any revival of utopian imagination in the near future, it cannot return to the old-style spatial utopias. New utopias would have to derive their form from the shifting and dissolving movement of society. They would not be rational cities evolved by a philosopher's dialectic; they would be rooted in the body as well as in the mind, in the unconscious as well as the conscious, in forests and deserts as well as in highways and buildings, in bed as well as in the symposium.[3]

Looking outward, we can ask if people in different cultures typically transpose their imaginary otherworlds to one of Manuel's three locations. Offhand I suggest that Confucian tradition is euchronian, in its vision of the once-and-future age of Yao and Shun. Indian tradition seems more attuned to eupsychia and the production of inner harmony. Japanese tradition—if we follow Nuita's interpretation—has been predominantly eutopian. Nuita relates this to the "visual" or "spatial" bias which threads through so many domains of Japanese life and which is best known from Japanese graphic arts. He also finds that Japanese utopian imagery embodies a "pictorial" sense of order, an asymmetric harmony that differs sharply from the mechanical order and symmetry of the usual Western utopia.

As further evidence of spatial bias, Nuita instances the way Japan twice used an actual-but-distant society as a model for self-transcendence: using T'ang China in this way in the eighth century, and the West in the nineteenth. To me, however, this kind of modeling is not uniquely Japanese. I see it in many culture-clash situations, especially where a people finds itself unable to cope with

[3] Ibid., pp. 346–47.

the allure and might of a vastly more developed civilization. Call it identification-with-the-aggressor if you wish, but many modernizing elites today—like the Japanese leaders of a century ago—hold an image of the future that is in large measure an image of what the West already has now.

Indeed, utopian visions often seem to be triggered by culture shock and the mind-stretch that comes with exposure to new forms of human otherness. Europeans went on a utopian binge after the voyages of discovery. Conversely, being confronted by outlandish Europeans, people around the world invented all manner of new alternative futures, ranging from humble Melanesian hopes for a great cargo ship to the more stately Chinese mansions of an elaborate construct like the *Ta-t'ung Shu*.[4] In Japan, as Nuita points out, an awareness of the West—seen at a distance through "Dutch Studies" and the few Dutch allowed to stay in Nagasaki—led some seventeenth-century Japanese writers such as Andō Shōeki to imagine Holland as a land of "natural order." And the opening of Japan to intense Western contact in the mid-nineteenth century loosed a utopian flood. Judging from the number of original books as well as translations that were published, Japanese of the 1880's and 1890's were as fond of reading and writing about utopia as were Westerners of the Bellamy era.[5]

You may balk at extending the term this way, if you are accustomed to thinking of utopia as some sort of fantasy of ultra-perfection. But it follows from the definition of utopia as a real-but-outlandish society that is used not only to criticize one's own world

[4] Kung-Chuan Hsiao, "In and out of Utopia: K'ang Yu-wei's Social Thought" (Seattle: University of Washington Far Eastern and Russian Institute, Modern Chinese History Project Reprint Series No. 31, 1969).

[5] See Sir George B. Sansom, *The Western World and Japan* (New York: Alfred Knopf, 1949), pp. 398–99, 415–20; Yoshie Okazaki, *Japanese Literature in the Meiji Era* (Tokyo: Ōbunsha, 1955), pp. 131–42; Izumi Yanagita, "Meiji Nihon no yūtopia shisō," *Sekai* (January 1964): 240–48.

but also to give positive guides for transforming it. Utopia need not promise ultimate perfection, so long as it offers a style of human completion—a way of life—better than any version available on the domestic cultural market. From this point of view, not only certain images of the future but also large chunks of historiography and ethnography need to be examined as forms of utopigraphy. The utopian motive may be close to the surface, as in Voltaire's use of Imperial China or Montaigne's descriptions of the Tupinamba. But even where it is submerged, as in much social science writing today, it seldom is absent and ought to be evaluated.

A concept needs to be stretched with care lest it become hollow. By bounding it with contrastive categories, we can begin to mark off what it is not. Nuita takes a step in this direction, opposing utopia to other forms of cultural rejection and self-criticism, such as satire and irony. Utopia to him is the highest form of criticism, since it reaches beyond mockery and nihilation to offer a way out. His approach might readily be expanded. Dystopias, for example— like *1984*—share the other features of utopias but differ in projecting an outland culture as a model to be shunned rather than emulated. Many forms of myth and science fiction offer criticism and "mirror" one's own world in the act of portraying fabulous otherworlds; they may not, however, furnish positive guides to self-transformation.

Nuita suggests a kind of linear relation between nihilation, satire, utopia, and the "strength of social barriers." This strikes me as the weakest part of his argument; it looks like too simple an instrument for untangling the complex roots of creativity, and it verges upon solipsism. Men envision utopias when the social barriers are strongest, he says; but the evidence that social barriers are at their strongest seems to be that men have envisioned utopias. One must have an independent measure of the strength of social barriers in order to establish a relationship of this kind. Perhaps in due course

Professor Nuita will propose such a measure, for his essay is but an occasional report on a comparative investigation which he has been pursuing for two decades; there is more to come.

Manuel looks mostly at content-motifs in his approach, Nuita at modes of criticism. George B. Bikle, Jr., takes up utopianism as a direction of thought and process of thinking. Bikle surveys some of the utopian motives that have been manifested during the shifting phases of Japan's century of modernization. Utopians, he points out, may often enough draw upon old notions of tribal simplicity or guild solidarity in shaping their previews of a transcending order. But he argues vigorously that this need not result in romantic flight from the social ills of industrial civilization, that in fact it can help make rational plans for overcoming modern *angst*.

Bikle finds this positive, or progressive, outlook in many domains of Japanese life in recent generations. On this count, Latin America offers contrast-value. For according to Joseph L. Love's interpretation—in the first section of Essay 6—utopian motives have been sporadic at best in Latin America and have most often been swamped by regressive impulses toward primitive rebellion.

Love's argument might, I fear, easily slip into social Darwinism: utopian image-work and utopian action-impulses have not become institutionalized on any large scale (pre-Castro?); therefore they are unfit for the modern Latin American environment. To me, one of the great virtues of Bikle's essay is that he contextualizes utopianism as one of a battery of Japanese responses to industrial dislocation, and that he is willing to grant that many of these responses were pregnant with creativity even though few of them gave birth to major institutions. Military ultra-nationalism won the day in the 1930's and suppressed all other forms. But its defeat and removal in 1945 opened the way for a remarkable surge of transforming energy. Important elements of utopianism came to the front, and the Occupation Era (1945–52) would be well worth examining with this in mind.

During conference discussions, Bikle and I both made a point that raised the hackles of some participants. We said that one should not shrink from looking for utopian motives also in Fascism and Japanism. To men of a generation that went to war against Fascism and Japanism, this smacks of treason. But I am simply trying to separate my own utopias from the concept of utopia as a tool for cultural analysis. Often the two remain fused, as in Fred Polak's definition of utopianism as "the art of the impossible as a long-run possibility, of visionary planning for a non-political society based on human altruism and solidarity."[6]

"The impossible as a long-run possibility, of visionary planning" is one way of phrasing the transcendent features of utopianism—though in these essays we are trying to define the features less poetically. But although my own utopia might partly be labeled a "non-political society based on human altruism and solidarity," I am sure that this would not hold for everybody's.

In one sense, this is the familiar dilemma of description versus prescription. Bikle favors the former; Nuita, the latter. Each stance has its virtues. Like Bikle, I happen to favor doing analysis and evaluation separately—though I insist that both are essential to the making of a complete, human, moral act—and prefer to relate a phenomenon, in the first instance, to its cultural context. I happen to think that both Fascism and Japanism had pretty feeble euchronias, as do our superstates today. Nevertheless, given their context, they did offer some transcending and positive images of the future. One can examine these for their positive worth and still reject means and tactics—like Buchenwald and Pearl Harbor—which were unarguably inhumane. Utopianism in this descriptive sense is not incompatible with tyranny. Djilas, in fact, equates the two and argues instead for envisioning an "unperfect" society. Nuita's essay is mostly descriptive, but his concept of utopia is colored by his own

[6] Fred Polak, *The Image of the Future* (New York: Oceana Press, 1960), Vol. 1, p. 426.

preferences. Thus he is obliged to argue that Fascist forms of utopianism were not "genuine." I grant that his position is consistent;
I fear, though, that it does not conduce to a very thorough understanding of how Fascism and Japanism were able to hold moral
sway over vast numbers of fellow humans.

Neither description nor prescription, defined narrowly, are good
labels for what James Allen Dator espouses so enthusiastically in the
third essay in this section. Dator is disturbed by the dearth and
weakness of utopian image-work in his own subculture of political
scientists. It is a concern that is being voiced increasingly, in various
forms and idioms, in scholarly symposia as well as in teach-ins and
demonstrations. It is a discontent with a sort of marginal-utility effect in social research, in which increments of precision seem to
yield decrements of prevision. Dator does not argue against the
descriptive control and use of explicit reasoning that are the hall-
marks of social science method. He simply asks why they cannot be
applied with equal vigor to looking forward as well as to looking
backward.

Now and again a social scientist has taken a fling at this kind of
descriptive previewing—witness B. F. Skinner's *Walden Two* or
Gabriel Tarde's *Underground Man*. But the great majority have
shied from it. Part of the difficulty stems from a vested interest in
the tribal gods: the "determinants" (such as institutions, culture,
personality, etc.) which give each discipline the Malinowskian
charter-myth that justifies its autonomy. To ask a political scientist
to describe a withering away of the state, or an anthropologist to
contemplate a withering away of culture, is asking him to commit
professional suicide. He has an understandable preference for stick-
ing to "surprise-free" projections (as they are known in RAND circles). Chairs of speculative philosophy, as is sometimes pointed out,
are few and far between in our academies.

Coupled with this, in the work of most social scientists, is a pen-
chant for being literal rather than literary, for analytic rather than

synthetic modes of thinking. There are counter-trends, though, in latter-day attention to "systems" and "ecology." More and more now, we get projections in the form of "scenarios" of a battery of linked variables. Computers are providing a boost to this kind of mind-stretch, as Dator mentions and as was discussed during the Illinois conference by Stuart Umpleby. So we have the beginnings of an art of forecasting complexity, a sort of second-level previewing. For third-level previewing, however, that sees beyond what is currently possible or likely, we still get no help from the scientists of man. In terms of Nuita's typology, the social scientist has not reached the stage of imagining utopias yet; he is still busy writing satire.

1. Traditional Utopias in Japan and the West: A Study in Contrasts

SEIJI NUITA
Yokohama National University

I

Ernst Toller states it well: "A man who cannot dream cannot live." Utopian thought, to me, is a manifestation of man's "en-

A preliminary version of this paper was given at the Conference on Utopia in Comparative Focus in May, 1968, and also was discussed that same month with members of the graduate seminar on cultural activism, Department of Anthropology, University of Illinois, Urbana. My thanks to those who, on both occasions, offered many helpful comments and criticisms.

I am grateful to Carol Link, Sei'ichi Makino, and David W. Plath for their work in translating this essay into English. And I am indebted

ergy of consciousness" as he pursues life.[1] This energy, needless to say, is not limited to utopian thought. Indeed, we may postulate stages in the development of thought in terms of the strength of this energy.

At the start of every stage, we always find despair. By despair, I mean the ultimate condition of man: faced with the certainty of a complete end of time—namely, with death—he aspires to the uncertainty that is life. Here the energy at work is existential. Kierkegaard's proposition that "you need infinite energy of mind if you intend to be yourself amidst despair" is a good description of the nature of this first energy of consciousness which man feels as he pursues life out of the depths of his despair.

Since despair is, put differently, the awareness of solitude, we may also say that the beginning of utopia lies in an awareness of solitude. Solitude in this context is the condemnation that falls precisely upon those who want to be truly free. Sartre states it in these terms: "We are alone, without excuses. This is what I mean when I say that man is condemned to be free. Condemned because he has not created himself, but on the other hand free because once he is thrown into the world he is responsible for whatever he does."[2]

In both Kierkegaard and Sartre, the energy of consciousness at this stage is manifested as existentialism itself. They ringingly declare their will to live. However, existentialism does not provide

---

to the Center for International Comparative Studies and the Department of Anthropology of the University of Illinois at Urbana for supporting my semester's research and study in that institution.

[1] The concept of energy of consciousness I am using here derives from ideas first set forth by Henri Bergson. He develops these in his first major work, *Essai sur les données immediates de la conscience* (1889, English version called *Time and Free Will*), and in a number of later essays collected and published in 1919 as *L'Énergie spirituelle, essais et conférences.*

[2] Jean-Paul Sartre, *L'Éxistentialisme est un humanisme* (Paris: Les Editions Nagel, 1965), p. 37.

us with an answer to the next crucial question, the question of *how* we should live.

If the energy of consciousness becomes stronger, it may produce a form of nihilism. This nihilism need not take on a negative character; it can be extremely positive, as exemplified in Nietzsche. Or again, the nihilists of Russia in the 1860's were capable of energetic social action. Some forms of nihilism can be called "negativism," as the Russian word implies. But dangerous as their goals may have been, both Nietzsche and the nihilists put their energy of consciousness into practice much more intensely than do most existentialists. If existentialism represents a powerful will to live, nihilism in its basic sense carries seeds of the creation of new life. But since nihilism offers no positive purpose for life, it too fails to answer the question of how we should live, no matter how strongly it motivates people to resist social barriers and to engage in destructive action.

At a still higher stage, where the energy of consciousness is curbed by strong social barriers, it sometimes develops into escapism. "Escape" may too easily be interpreted to mean some sort of feeble failure. But if, for example, a humanist elects to become an outsider to his society rather than cooperate with inhumane leaders and organizations, the energy of consciousness has risen to provide great strength.

What happens when social barriers are overwhelming? Then the only weapon available to a man may be fable or satire. Using the energy of consciousness to produce satire may seem, superficially, a weaker response than that of nihilism. But I believe that if a man's only recourse is to satire, that is evidence that the social barriers are more powerful for him than for the nihilist.

In short, I am arguing that the energy of consciousness as manifested at each stage—existentialism, nihilism, escapism, fable, satire—is a picture of man's resistance to the inhumane barriers of society.

But there is yet another manifestation of this energy, this ultimate energy of human life. In this manifestation, man jumps over the social barriers in order to attack them from the other side. This is utopia. Utopia in this sense is the greatest of the expressions of man's energy of consciousness. To me utopia is not some simple daydream. There are, to be sure, many utopias that are simplistic. But the problem to be pursued is that of the ground from which utopias grow. According to the perspective I am proposing here—that of stages of manifestation for the energy of consciousness—we should look for, as the birthground of utopian visions, human conditions as severe and critical as, indeed, more severe and critical than, those that resulted in existentialism or nihilism.

I I

In my own studies, then, I begin with a definition of utopia as the greatest of all the manifestations of man's energy of consciousness. I try to analyze and compare individual utopias, identifying in them the interrelationships of the constituent elements of the life-energy that is within human consciousness. Every utopia reflects its age and environment, of course, illustrating their unique forms of content and expression. One could write an extremely interesting and unique history of world civilization from this point of view, tracing the manner in which the people of each nation aspired to life at a given age. But in my own work I am more concerned with finding those elements of the energy of consciousness which are common to every utopia, regardless of era, race, or nationality. By extracting these common elements, I hope I can eventually add a little concreteness to our hitherto only vaguely defined notions of human nature. If this can be done, I believe we may go on to establish subsidiary criteria for the behavioral sciences, among other fields of study.

This is work in process, but I do want to make one point in this regard. The constituents of human nature—of the energy of consciousness that aspires to live—cannot be reduced to one or two elements in the core of consciousness, any more than elemental particles of matter can be reduced to one substance. Human nature is a synthesis of several mutually contradictory, heterogeneous elements. So the more we try to reduce the essence of human nature to one or another element, the more we transform consciousness into something inhuman. If we do that, as Nazi theory did, for example,[3] we end with a view of consciousness as something powerful but limited—as though the symphony orchestra of mankind consisted of nothing but trombones. I do not see that this kind of view can provide an ultimate grounding for the behavioral sciences: it neglects the wider meaning of the energy of consciousness, and I believe that inherent energy is what determines value. This is the ultimate goal of my studies of utopia.

[3] True utopian thought is diametrically opposed to the ideologies of Nazism and Fascism. The difference will be clear if we start with the energy of consciousness. Hitler, for example, says in *Mein Kampf* that "A fox is a fox, a tiger a tiger, and a goose a goose. Just as cats never like rats, so geese never love foxes." Traditional studies of man have argued against such a line of reasoning, insisting that man is essentially different from other animals.

From the standpoint of the energy of consciousness, Hitler is not all wrong; a fox is a fox. But the theory lacks logic. For any theory, one must formally establish a relation between minimum and maximum units; otherwise the theory becomes indiscriminate. If one thinks, following Hitler, in terms of a homogeneous species such as fox or goose as the minimum unit, then the maximum unit can be nothing but a homogeneous people or nation. A true utopia will take nothing less than mankind as its maximum unit. This is what Martin Buber means when he writes that "the primary aspiration of all history is a genuine community of human beings—genuine because it is *community all through*" (*Paths in Utopia*, p. 133).

I I I

Thomas More coined the term "utopia," of course, but similar ideas can be traced far back into antiquity. If we are considering the history of utopian thought from a world viewpoint, we certainly cannot disregard the utopias of the ancient Orient,[4] of China and of other countries. Strictly speaking, I feel that, outside the West, only in China do you find a tradition of typical utopian thinking that continues from ancient to modern times. Outside of China we find only sporadic examples. Ancient India, for instance, created a perfect, spatial image of utopia in Buddhism's Pure Land of Eternal Happiness. But typical utopias—if we use the West as the type-case—did not arise in later periods of Indian history.[5] In Japan, too, we have several early examples of utopian thinking; however, if one measures them strictly, in terms of stages of the energy of consciousness, they have to be classified mostly as satire. Today in Japan there is great interest in futurology; before long it will be an independent field of study. But at the moment it strikes me as being little more than a theory of economic growth and of prediction by scientific extrapolation. Futurology differs from utopia in that it lacks a thoroughly critical attitude toward society.

The Chinese utopias are very similar in type to Western ones

[4] The following recent work is noteworthy since it does not simply ascribe the sources of utopianism to Hellenism and Judaism but includes the older utopian ideas of the Orient: Neil Eurich, *Science in Utopia; A Mighty Design* (Cambridge: Harvard University Press, 1967).

[5] Later in the essay, I cite the *Sukhāvati-vyūha* of the Three Sutras of the Pure Land as one good example of an Indian utopia. If we regard the spiritual kingdoms of the Buddha as a source of utopian thought, then the *Tripitaka* and the *Saddharma-pundarika sutra* also take on great importance.

and deserve much further investigation along comparative lines. But in what follows I am going to deal mainly with Japanese utopias, since they offer the novelty of greater contrast with those of the West. This will, at the same time, allow me to sketch a utopian tradition that probably is not familiar to most of you.

IV

If we take utopia to be a manifestation of the energy of consciousness, we can use it as a parameter of civilization. Now, the word civilization is derived from Latin words for city and citizen; etymologically, civilization is the art of constructing cities. In turn, we may say that one primary feature of utopian thinking is the modification of nature by man. Nature and natural scenery, no matter how mysterious or beautiful, cannot be utopias. Utopia is thoroughly artificial in that it always originates in human plans and challenges the environment, transforming nature to improve it for human habitation.

Western society has a consistent tradition of natural law from ancient times onward, and in Western utopias we always find an obvious confrontation between man and nature. The Japanese view of nature is different. In Japanese tradition, from ancient ages to the present, people have accepted nature rather obediently. Even now Japanese daily life, even in high-rise urban apartments, is permeated with references to flowers and winds, the moon and the changing seasons. That is, Japanese continue to give spiritual value to the beauty of nature; in doing so, they maintain their form of higher spirituality, as evidenced in the excellence of Japanese arts.

Where does this Japanese view of nature come from? This is a mammoth problem, but I would draw your attention to one basic point. You will not find, at the core of Japanese thought, a Bible governing a strict oppositional relationship between man and nature; rather, you will find the spirit of *waka* poetry. Consciousness of original sin—consciousness of the primordial solitude that comes when man is severed from nature—does not underlie thinking in Japan as in the West.

The oldest extant Japanese book is the *Kojiki* (ca. 712 A.D.), which in a loose sense is a sort of mythology. Its author describes how the ancestral gods of the imperial family created the land, and how their descendants came to rule it. Nominally a tale about gods, actually it tells much about politics during the establishment of an ancient state. This is a far cry from mythology in the Western sense, in which *mythos* is always opposed to *doxa*. *Mythos* in the Western sense contains a bud that will blossom in utopia, but Japanese god-tales lack this source.

I believe that the Japanese style of thinking arises more directly from the tradition of the *Man'yōshū*. This was the first great collection of *waka* poems, published in the middle of the eighth century A.D. The *waka* tradition has continued without interruption since well before the eighth century as an expression of the most refined spiritual life of the imperial family and of aristocratic circles. Even now on every New Year's Day the poems of the imperial family are made public, and at the same time the general populace volunteers poems on a theme set by the emperor.

It is no exaggeration to say that the main themes in the *Man'-yōshū* are love and the four seasons. The seasons are fairly distinct in a Japanese year, each with its own natural beauty. Most Japanese have an intimate feeling toward the vicissitudes of the seasons and nurture subtle sensitivity toward them, all the while feeling the delicateness of nature. Here nature is never an object to be challenged by man. In poetry, for example, love between a man and a woman usually is projected into nature and expressed by phrases such as "I weep watching flowers," "I weep watching the moon," "I cry in my heart feeling the wind and the dew." When man and nature fuse in this way, there is no seed for the growth of a vision of utopia as human artifice.

From tenth-century Japan, we have one literary work that has utopian elements in it, although it is not a full manifestation of utopian energy.

This is the *Taketori monogatari*, or *Tale of the Bamboo Cutter*. Briefly, the story runs as follows: Long, long ago there was an old man who made his living by cutting bamboo. One day, between the joints of a bamboo stalk, he found a girl three inches high. He brought her home and began raising her, and in about three months she had become a full-grown and beautiful young woman. Five noblemen came, one after another, and proposed to her, but she threw them a challenge. Each was sent to seek rare and precious goods; each failed. The emperor also proposed to her and also was refused. The story ends with her saying, "Let's go to the town in the moon." In short, for all the ego-strength and imagination in the story, it ends with the heroine's return to the moon. The consciousness of self manifested here is not strong enough to project the self to the moon and depict a new life, as would be the case in a typical Western utopia.

V

It is not until the eighteenth century that we find in Japanese thinking an awareness of opposition between man and nature. At that time, two important utopias were written with this kind of awareness: *Shizen shin'eidō* (1775), by Andō Shōeki (1701–58?), and *Fūryū Shidōken den* (1763), by Hiraga Gennai (pseudonym Fūrai Sanjin, 1726–79).

Andō is called the Rousseau of Japan. He denounced the caste system of the feudal Japan of his day and went on to propose a better form. In Chapter 25 of *Shizen shin'eidō*, you will find a section entitled "Theory of the Natural World," in which he sketches an ideal society in which every man will equally cultivate the land. Strictly speaking, man does not challenge nature, in Andō's view; but he does need to harmonize with it.

Andō refers to his ideal society as *shizensei*, "the natural order." In it there is harmony between man and nature by dint of *jikikō* or direct cultivation of the soil. Andō contrasts this with *hōsei*, "the legal order," the society in which man makes laws as he pleases and thus strays from rapport with nature. Feudal society, he said, was a legal order and therefore basically contrary to the laws of nature.

In his society based on natural order, people of the plains would provide grain; people of the mountains, wood; and people of the seacoast, fish. Natural resources are distributed in all three environments, so there should be neither rich nor poor people. And, with no caste differences, superiors will not persecute inferiors and inferiors will not need to flatter superiors. Thus people will not bear grudges, quarrel, or fight. With everybody equal, there will be no egoistic teaching, no distinction between the wise and the foolish. Since no one will teach them about being dutiful or not being dutiful, children will neither hate their parents nor flatter them. Parents in turn will neither hate their children nor dote upon them.[6]

Interestingly enough, Andō believed that his "natural order" already was in existence in Ezo (Hokkaido) and in Holland, which he thought was an island country like Japan. He visited Nagasaki frequently, got acquainted with the Dutch stationed there, and through them came to know a little about European life, at least in its Dutch version. This seems to be characteristic

[6] The standard work in English on Andō is E. H. Norman's monograph, "Andō Shōeki and the Anatomy of Japanese Feudalism," *Transactions of the Asiatic Society of Japan*, 3rd ser., Vol. 2 (1949).

of Japanese utopian thinking: the model is not $u + topos$, or *no-place*, but often is thought to already exist in some distant place. This struggle to approach or even surpass an idealized nation already in existence is a familiar theme in Japanese history. It has much to do with the process of Japan's modernization, especially with Japanese nationalism, for it is at the heart of nationalistic thought as that emerges in the late Tokugawa and early Meiji periods.[7]

As E. H. Norman pointed out, Andō seems to be "the only person among Japanese men of thought before the Meiji era" who relentlessly criticized the feudal system. However, Andō did not engage in direct reform action; he was content to suggest changes. On this count his utopianism resembles that of mid-seventeenth-century Britain. I am thinking of books such as Samuel Hartlib's *A Description of the Famous Kingdom of Macaria* (1641), Gerrard Winstanley's *The Law of Freedom in a Platform* (1652), and James Harrington's famous *The Com-mon-Wealth of Oceana* (1656). In general these books are tinged with deism and natural science, and their outlook reflects that of the age of the English revolution. They do not offer grand schemes so much as direct guides to political and social reform. Absolutism was under attack; ideas of natural law and communism were coming to the fore, and even being acted upon directly by the Diggers.

In the Japan of Andō's time, contradictions in the feudal system were rapidly manifesting themselves. The petite bourgeoisie controlled the economy in the advanced areas of the country, and even the self-supporting backward areas were tied in to the

---

[7] With regard to this and other characteristics of early Japanese nationalism in the modern era, see Masao Maruyama's essay, "Nationalism in Japan: Its Theoretical Background and Prospects," Ch. 4 of his *Thought and Behaviour in Modern Japanese Politics* (New York: Oxford University Press, 1963).

mercantile system. Feudal lords were pressed by increasing expenses and tried to cover their debts by raising taxes. Peasants suffered heavily from taxation and from landlord control, and when they rebelled they were persecuted severely. Bad weather resulted in famine. In the worst famine, that of 1732, some 2.6 million peasants are said to have starved to death. In short, the feudal order showed symptoms of a systemic crisis.

In other words, eighteenth-century Japan, like seventeenth-century Britain, was an age of social concussion. In both countries, men apparently were convinced, first, that reforms were possible, and second, that criticism would not necessarily result in punishment. The implication I draw from this is that where conditions are identical or at least closely similar, we should expect no vast differences in the kind of utopias that are produced, whether East or West. Only when a trapped consciousness is forced back upon the core of its native tradition of thought are we likely to see utopias with conspicuous cultural differences.

V I

Hiraga Gennai is noted in Japan more for his inventions than for his literary works. He had a keen interest in many phenomena, studying their underlying principles and then applying these to technology. He is especially famous for an electromotor which he invented in 1776. Like Andō and others in all modern fields of study at the time, Hiraga also went to Nagasaki to learn from the Dutch.[8]

In the eyes of a talented man like Hiraga, who early mastered

[8] Little or nothing on Hiraga is available in Western languages. He also was one of the first Japanese to dabble with oil-painting techniques imported from the West in the eighteenth century. An oil painting ascribed to him is reprinted facing p. 238 of Sir George B. Sansom's *The Western World and Japan* (New York: Knopf, 1950).

a number of fields of science, most Japanese scholars and intellectuals looked silly. He expressed this in several works of fiction with unusual titles, one of these being *Fūryū Shidōken den,* or *The Romantic Biography of Shidōken.* In this he makes a hero of Shidōken Fukai, an actual person who was a professional storyteller in the Asakusa district of Edo (now Tokyo). As the hero travels, he sees and hears different facets of life in feudal Japan, which Hiraga describes satirically. Hiraga goes on with imagination and hyperbole, sketching various fictional worlds —the land of big people, the land of dwarfs, the land of women, and so on. He relentlessly satirizes sham and deception.

One cannot help but think of *Gulliver's Travels.* It was written in 1726, almost forty years before *Shidōken;* chronologically, direct influence was possible, although it remains to be proved. It is possible that Hiraga was introduced to *Gulliver* by Dutch scholars, although the first (and partial) translation of *Gulliver* into Japanese did not come until 1880. More likely, Hiraga derived his ideas from Chinese writings about fantastic lands.

In terms of the stages I postulated earlier, *Shidōken* is satire and pre-utopian. However, Hiraga's book is important in that it stimulated a number of utopian writings in subsequent generations. Two good examples are Yūkokushi's *Ikoku kidan, Wasōbyōe* (1774), and Bakin's *Musōbyōe, kochō monogatari* (1809–10).

We know nothing about Yūkokushi's life, but his *Wasōbyōe,* or *Strange Tales of Foreign Lands,* seems to have been very much influenced by Hiraga. The protagonist Wasōbyōe lived in Nagasaki and was a dealer in Chinese imports. In mid-August one year, he was coasting in a small boat when he was blown away by a typhoon. He drifted at sea for about three months, until he arrived at the land of eternal youth and immortality. There he lived for 200 years, until he tired of it and went instead to the land of freedom. He also went to visit the land of vanity, the land of love of antiquities, the land of desperation, etc., etc. The author uses each land as a fresh platform for satirizing his own society.[9]

A second part was published in 1779. In it the hero, riding on a tortoise, visited still other lands—of cleanliness, of long legs, of cunning and stinginess, of boldness; and finally the land of women, where he awoke from his sleep as soon as he tried to escape. Artistically this second part is much inferior to the first, and most scholars believe it was written by a different hand.

Bakin is widely respected in Japanese literary history, and *Musōbyōe, the Tale of a Wanderer*, is but one of his many works. Musōbyōe, a fisherman, goes in his dreams to visit another array of unusual lands—of avarice, of grief, of sex, of heavy drinking. But instead of merely satirizing feudal Japan, Bakin uses the literary vehicle to develop his own outlook. Born into a warrior family, he was more attuned to caste differences and to Bushido than were many other writers of the day. But he was obliged to earn his living at the despised craft of fiction writing. His inner strife drove him to produce satire of a sort, but the satire is directed against himself more than against society at large.

I hope that I have amply illustrated what I asserted earlier: that traditional Japanese utopias do not fit the Western model but remain instead at the stage of satire. Let me amplify on why I think this is so.

It is sometimes said that Japan was under a feudal rule so rigid that people were unable to criticize society and could do no more than divert themselves with parody and satire. In a loose and general way, it may be true that the majority of the populace

[9] For a translation of the sections on "The Land of Perennial Life" and "The Land of the Giants," see B. H. Chamberlain, "Wasōbyōe, the Japanese Gulliver," *Transactions of the Asiatic Society of Japan*, 1st ser., Vol. 6, Pt. 4 (1879):287–313.

did not openly attack the feudal order. But I disagree with the general line of reasoning. I believe that usually, in any nation, the stronger the social barriers, the more spectacular will be the utopias that appear. Bushido is not a servile philosophy, and the Japanese are not a servile people.

My argument can always be reduced to my view of stages in the manifestation of the energy of consciousness. From that point of view, there is no question of the Japanese lacking enough energy to give birth to utopian visions. Rather, I claim that the Japanese tradition of social thought has not been rooted in the problem of the consciousness of solitude which is, I believe, essential to the birth of utopias. Man is not separated from nature, nor need he confront it, in the traditional Japanese outlook.

VII

A second major feature of the typical Western utopia is its concern for human liberation and freedom. Western thought always is rooted in an acute consciousness of solitude and a deep concern for the problem of free will. It continues to be a major issue at the bottom of every branch of learning and theory and has of course long been a central issue in religion. One might argue that religion is the same as utopia, in that both are among the highest manifestations of the energy of consciousness as it pursues life.

But is this correct? Religion and utopia do resemble each other, but I see a basic difference. Both are visions of rightness. But, as Martin Buber phrases it in *Paths in Utopia*, religion is "the vision of rightness in revelation," whereas utopia is "the vision of rightness in the Ideal." The energy of consciousness in religion "is realized in the picture of a perfect time—as messianic eschatology," but in utopia it "is realized in the picture of a perfect space."[10]

Thus the Kingdom of God in religion remains spiritual; in utopia, we are concerned with design and form. Utopia and religion may be in harmony, but often religion regards utopia as heresy. So long as a religion accepts free will, as does Judaism, the religious canons may remain as utopias. Early Catholics, too, generally accepted free will and often considered utopia to be the Kingdom of God. But with the passing of time, grace came to be emphasized and free will rejected. When Erasmus criticized Luther from the Catholic viewpoint by writing *De Libero Arbitrio*, Luther responded with *De Servo Arbitrio*. As Protestants took hegemony in the post-Reformation world, utopias based on free will came to be regarded as obvious heresy.

In Islam, too, the problem of free will has an important bearing upon utopian thinking. The Muslim majority was inclined to reject free will in the early years after the death of Mohammed, but before long Syrian scholars (the Qadarites) began to criticize this outlook. As Greek philosophies were introduced, fatalism came under attack, and "reason" came to hold authority. Interpretations of the *Koran* became theoretical, and a doctrine of the undeniable existence of free will was formulated.

Utopian thinking in the Islamic world first appears in twelfth-century Persia in the *Rubaiyat* of Omar Khayyam. There is, to be sure, no spatial image of an ideal world in the poem. But underlying the world depicted in it is an acute consciousness of opposition between man and nature, of the problem of free will, of the solitude that comes with a knowledge of human limits— all depicted with precision. In other words, he portrays a kingdom of free will.

In the mental climate of traditional Japan, the problem of free

[10] Martin Buber, *Paths in Utopia* (Boston: Beacon Press, 1958), p. 8.

will was not taken so seriously as in the West. The implication I draw from this is that, in Japan, solitude does not arise from primordial human nature but from the nature of everyday actual living. Japanese satires and political novels do criticize society; and since they do pursue a more ideal and more humanized social mold, they should be considered as forms of utopia. However, the Japanese attitude is so closely bound to ordinary routine living that it runs a great danger. If the goal is simply to improve daily life and there is no attempt to grasp humanity in its fullness, one may eventually become obsessed with efficiency. History teaches us that undue pursuit of efficiency on the level of actual, instinctual life can easily slide into rigid determinism, as in Fascism and Nazism.[11]

VIII

The third characteristic of a typical utopia is symmetry. This, too, is based upon an oppositional relationship between nature and man. It implies both a reasoned conquest of nature and a reasoned design for a new social order. Utopian designs, unlike ordinary construction plans, are based upon a spirit of equality; and, as a picture of space, utopia contains important elements of symmetry, such as bisymmetry. Typical Western utopias have a surprisingly symmetrical shape.

Some Eastern utopias also are symmetrical; a good example can

[11] Concerning the utopias of Nazism, see Paul Dupays, *Utopie hitlérienne en France; chronique historique, août-septembre 1940* (Editions de la Critique; depositaire a Londres, Hachette, 1951). Also John R. Bengtson, *Nazi War Aims: The Plan for the Thousand Year Reich* (Rock Island, Ill.: Augustana College Library, 1962). With regard to utopias of Fascism, Mussolini himself published a journal called *Utopia*. It was first issued in 1913 and apparently continued for a year, up to No. 18, although there are many combined numbers. Some of the issues are available in the Harvard University Library.

be found in Indian tradition. The most significant of the Indian utopias is the Pure Land of Eternal Happiness, found in the sutra called the *Larger Sukhāvati-vyūha.* If you look into the paradise depicted there, you find a temple surrounded by sevenfold stone walls. Various trees made of seven jewels are ranged symmetrically; symmetrical, too, are their branches, leaves, flowers, and fruits. The great lotus pond measures the same in breadth, length, and depth; inside this cubic pond are regular sets of stairs. In short, there is geometrical symmetry throughout.

In Japan, by contrast, this symmetry is transformed. The beauty of harmony is manifested in *pictorial* rather than geometrical symmetry. The cubic lotus pond becomes simply a beautiful pond in a Japanese garden. It is true that the city of Kyoto, Japan's ancient capital, was planned with geometric symmetry. But the plan was borrowed from Ch'ang-an, the T'ang dynasty capital. Thus Japan differs from Indian and Chinese traditions, which share with the West a concern for symmetry. Japan's famed graphic arts derive from this concern for pictorial rather than geometric symmetry; at the same time, this concern seems to have blocked the growth of typical utopias.

I X

As Japan entered her modern era in the mid-nineteenth century, a flood of utopias began to arise. In style and in method, these works are obviously much influenced by Western models, as was all of Japan at the time. The focus was on establishing a modern nation, and the critical spirit—to me, the taproot of utopianism—was weak. Most of the utopias of the period were political novels close to actual conditions, which sketched alternative futures for Japanese (and sometimes world) government.

It was similar to today's futurology in many respects, but oriented to politics rather than to economics.

The first year of the modern era (1868) also saw the first translation of a Western utopian work into Japanese. This was the book by the Dutch author Dioscorides (Alexander V. W. Bikkers, 1812–85) entitled *Anno 2065: een Blik in de Toekomst, door Dr. D. Tweede druk*, originally published at Utrecht in 1865. Its Japanese version bore the title *Zen sekai mirai ki*, or *An Account of the World's Future*. More's *Utopia* itself was translated in 1882, and during the Meiji period as a whole (1868–1912), some three dozen other works also appeared in translation—Fenélon, Verne, Bellamy, Bulwer-Lytton, etc.

I cannot hope to cover all the utopias of the Meiji period, so let me give just a few examples. It was in 1889 that the first modern national constitution was promulgated. In the following year, Japan held her first general election and inaugurated a national parliament. A few years before that, political utopias had had a vogue. The first ones were Takase Naokuni's *Nijūsan-nen mirai ki* (*An Account of the Future Twenty-third Year*), which appeared in 1883, and a book of the very same title written by Suehiro Shigeyasu and published in May, 1886.

"Twenty-third year" meant the twenty-third year of the reign of the Meiji emperor, which would be 1890. Suehiro's work sold 300,000 copies. Its success stimulated Hattori Sei'ichi's *Nijūsan-nen rokkai mirai ki* (*Report on the National Diet in the Future Twenty-third Year*), which appeared in October of the same year. Hattori was prolific as a utopianist. Among his other writings were a sequel to Bakin, entitled *Dainisei Musobyōe kochō monogatari* (1884), *Nijisseiki shin-ajia* (*New Asia in the Twentieth Century*) in 1887, and others as well.[12]

[12] For a few sketchy remarks on some of the Meiji era political and utopian novels, see Yoshie Okazaki, *Japanese Literature in the Meiji Era* (Tokyo, 1955), pp. 131–42, and Sir George B. Sansom, *The Western*

X

I have tried, in the preceding sections, to contrast some basic features of Western and Japanese traditional utopias. I would like, in concluding, to pose a problem that I am unable to resolve.

World and Japan, pp. 398–99, 415–20. I append a list of utopias from Tokugawa and Meiji Japan, so far as I have been able to discover to date:

1775   Andō Shōeki: *Shizen shin'eidō.*
1763   Hiraga Gennai (Fūrai Sanjin, pseud.): *Fūryū Shidōken-den.*
1774   Yūkokushi (pseud.): *Ikoku kidan; Wasōbyōe.*
1809 & 1810   Takizawa Bakin (Kyokutei Bakin, pseud.): *Musōbyōe kochō monogatari.*
1880   Furaishi (pseud.): *Kurogai yume monogatari.*
1880   Kishi Jinsaku: *Kukusei musoki.*
1883   Takase Naoaki: *Nijūsen-nen miraiki.*
1884   Hattori Sei'ichi: *Dainisei Musōbyōe kochō monogatari.*
1885–97   Shiba shirō (Tokai Sanshi, pseud.): *Kajin no kigu.*
1886   Tsubouchi Shōyō: *Naichi zakkyo mirai no yume.*
1886   Suehiro Shigeyasu (Suehiro Tetchō, pseud.): *Nijūsan-nen miraiki.*
1886   Hattori Sei'ichi: *Nijūsan-nen kokkai miraiki.*
1886   Suehiro Shigeyasu (Suehiro Tetchō, pseud.): *Setchūbai.*
1886   Sudō Nansui: *Shinshō no kajin.*
1886   Tokutomi I'ichirō (Tokutomi Soho, pseud.): *Shōrai no Nippon.*
1886   Sugiura Jūgo: *Hankai yume monogatari.*
1887   Senkyo Sanshi: *Kokkaigo no Nippon.*
1887   Ushiyama Kadudō: *Nippon no shōrai.*
1887   Hattori Sei'ichi: *Nijusseiki shin Ajia.*
1887   *Seitetsu yume monogatari.*
1887   Yoneyama Shōshi: *Meiji nijūsan-nen Musōbyōe kaimei monogatari.*
1887   Suehiro Shigeyasu (Suehiro Tetchō, pseud.): *Kakanwō.*
1887   Uchimura Yoshishirō: *Nijūsan-nen mugenshō.*
1887   Tokutomi I'ichirō (Tokutomi Soho, pseud.): *Shin Nippon no seinen.*
1890   Yano Fumio (Yano Ryūkei, pseud.): *Ukishiro monogatari.*
1893   Suehiro Shigeyasu (Suehiro Tetchō, pseud.): *Meiji yonjū-nen no Nippon.*
1893   Morimoto Tokichi: *Daitō gappōron.*
1902   Miyazaki Toten: *Sanjūsan-nen no yume.*
1902   Yano Fumio (Yano Ryūkei, pseud.): *Shin shakai.*

Utopia can be used as a barometer to measure the life-energy of a nation; if a race or a people lives vigorously in world history, it will produce utopias befitting its vigor. As I want to extract some guiding principles for behavioral science from the constitutent features of utopias, I am concerned about Eastern utopias. My question is whether there is in Eastern utopias—Chinese ones excepted, perhaps—enough creative energy to produce a new civilization. The period in which the Indian Pure Land of Eternal Happiness appeared was the era in which the Kushana dynasty and trading system were at their peak. Islamic utopias, the age during which Islamic civilization spread across vast areas from Persia through Spain, appeared in the twelfth through fourteenth centuries. To me, it is not enough to view utopias as simple reflections of a cultural system. But these Eastern utopias seem mainly to be reflections of the greatness of their own cultures at that time. I find it difficult to discover the dynamic energy of life in them. And this is puzzling, because I believe that a genuine utopia is rooted in our human sense of solitude and our deepest desire for the humanly human life.

2. Utopianism and the Planning Element in Modern Japan

GEORGE B. BIKLE, JR.
University of California, Riverside

I

My own interest in utopianism derives from my research into the social thought of a great Asian Christian, Kagawa Toyohiko. To my surprise, I discovered that the utopian theme was the one constant thread that ran through all of Kagawa's writings on social reform, from his first indignant letter to the editor of the *Tokushima Mainichi News* protesting the inhumanity of the Russo-Japanese War, to the writings immediately before his death in the late 1950's on the need for world peace and brotherhood. I became convinced that what we call utopianism can only with difficulty be separated from the broader problem of Japanese religion, and moreover, at least in the case of a paracletic like Kagawa, the common Western stereotypes of other-worldly retreatism would aptly fit neither his mysticism nor his utopianism. These thoughts led me to speculate about the social psychology of Kagawa's religious approach to the world and the unique manner in which he rationalized these attitudes into a secular utopian-reform mission. In the end, because of the singular role this man played in the founding of Japanese social movements during years of intense industrial crisis, I began to entertain the possibility that the particular brand of utopianism Kagawa espoused was not retreatist in inspiration, but world-embracing and constructive and compatible with the ends of Japanese modernization. Indeed, the industrial democracy Kagawa projected for his proletarian comrades, though inimical to capitalism, was a perfectly feasible alternative for rapidly modernizing Japan of the Taisho-Showa era.

These, however, are merely introductory remarks. I wish to comment upon Japanese utopianism in much broader perspective. I will take up the contribution indigenous systems of thought may have made to the rise of a planning tradition during the Tokugawa period, the confluence of this native interest in planning with imported forms of utopian socialism during late Meiji, and the possible role of utopian planning in this new synthetic form during the height of Japanese industrialization. All the following remarks are offered in a speculative spirit as possible avenues of approach to the problem of utopianism in a modernizing non-Western context.

II

Utopianism can be defined as any process of thought expressed in the form of concepts, symbols, fantasies, dreams, or ideas which does not arise directly out of social reality, yet aims to change the present state of things to conform to the transcendent vision it projects.[1] Often it is the social visionary or prophet who mystically fuses the unreal subjective and symbolic wish-fulfillment fictions of a group, sect, or social class with the datum of objective reality to herald an ideal world spatially or temporally removed from the disintegrating social order observed about him. If we accept this definition, utopianism certainly is nothing new, for we can discern such transilient projections in the teachings of the Hebrew prophets, the messianic visions of Christ, the self-searchings of the medieval monastic contemplatives, the millenarian social protests of the pre-Reformation paracletics, the gnosticism of the English pietists, the separatism of the early nineteenth-century communitarians, the schemes for reform of the English laborites; and even today this ever-present longing to retreat into the communal womb abounds among myriads of utopian sects in our modern, technologically advanced societies. Thus clear evidence of the utopian mentality is liberally sprinkled across the pages of modern history.

The persistence of utopian modes of thinking through time raises the interesting question of the relationship of such future-oriented movements to the historical process itself. The question is not unrelated to the problem of primitivism and its persistence into the present. Truly, as scholars we are reluctant to believe that the desire to retreat into pre-modern, communal forms could have survived the so-called "primitive transformation." But if we are troubled by the ability of the utopian mentality to survive the leap from primitivism to more sophisticated institutional organizational forms, research into the nature of the industrial revolution makes us equally reluctant to believe that primordial

[1] Karl Mannheim, "Utopia," in E. A. Seligman and A. Johnson, eds., *Encyclopedia of Social Sciences*, vol. 15 (New York: Macmillan, 1935), p. 201.

modes of fanticization could have weathered the qualitative changes many of us assume accompanied the transition to capitalism and a modern technological order. This question is raised all the more fully by the Marxists who, smug in the certainty of "scientific socialism," have labeled all utopian forms of socialism as heresies. So successful have they been that today "utopian" conjures up visions of irrational flight from the alleged evils of machine civilization and befuddled attempts to resuscitate bizarre phases of outmoded communalism.[2]

But these Marxian polemics raise an important question: Can we unequivocally accept Engels's disdainful dismissal of the schemes of Fourier, Proudhon, and St. Simon as utopian in the retrogressive sense? Or must we examine such utopian projections more closely, with the caveat before us that the historical situations out of which they arose, and the questions to which they were addressed, were not those postulated by utopians today? To state the issue more succinctly, if the qualitative transformation we have assumed really did accompany modernization in the West, would not such changes have affected the utopian mentality as well? I suggest that the varieties of utopian experience cannot be divorced from the historical situations in which they arose and that, therefore, those modes of utopian spatialization which have manifested themselves in response to industrialization must be viewed in terms of the problems raised by the modernization process itself. Only if we admit the relativity of utopian movements to the historical age in which they were spawned will we be able to evolve meaningful definitions and ideal types.

One careful reexamination of the changes that forms of utopianism have undergone in their journey through time can be found in Martin Buber's *Paths in Utopia*. With Buber we are

[2] Martin Buber, *Paths in Utopia* (Boston: Beacon Press, 1958), p. 5.

prepared to argue that flight into archaic modes of communalism may have characterized the schemes for social reform of many nineteenth-century socialists in the West, but that by the turn of the twentieth century the pasting of utopian labels upon such forward-looking social movements as the Scandinavian coopera-tives, which were proving perfectly compatible with moderniza-tion, had to be undertaken with a great deal more care. In many cases, as Buber convincingly showed, the utopian imagination in-corporated a hard-headed element of rational planning which, far from proposing world-rejecting flight, actually thrust for-ward thoughtful programs for social reorganization which were perfectly capable of realization in the not-too-distant future.[3]

Buber's interpretation possesses interesting possibilities when we come to examine the conditions under which forms of uto-pian thought were imported into such non-Western contexts as rapidly modernizing Japan. If, for example, the mode of utopian thought introduced contained that planning element described by Buber, is it not possible that, rather than serving to assuage the anxieties raised by the impact of machine technology upon the traditional order, such forms of utopianism might actually have provided ideological support for those special types of ra-tionality Weber suggested underlay the emergence of modern capitalism?[4] In other words, I suggest that those entrepreneurial modes of thought that seek to manipulate available means to achieve economic ends do not differ in essence from the prac-tical proposals for institutional reform proffered by the utopian seer. True, this need not be the case. Often the social visionary will forswear the role of technocrat and social engineer, prefer-ring to appeal to the intervention of supernatural forces or the ineluctable operation of natural law to bring the prophesied ends

[3] Ibid., pp. 11–15.
[4] Max Weber, *The Protestant Ethic and the Spirit of Capitalism* (New York: Charles Scribner's Sons, 1958).

to pass. But the closer we approach to the turn of the twentieth century, the more frequently this seems *not* to have been the case. Beneath the rhetoric of the utopian's prophetic plea, we can find evidence of that hard-headed thread of means-ends planning which Weber found essential, along with other attitudes, to the rise of modern capitalism.

Nevertheless, certain obstacles may prevent the successful development of this theme. After all, Weber's so-called *Zwecksrationalitat* was a mode of thought adduced to explain how the entrepreneur manipulates his environment in order to accumulate capital, while the utopian mentality supposedly arises in response to the evils of capitalism. The utopian's fundamental abhorrence of capitalism would seem to militate against any further elaboration of this hypothesis. Yet I believe there is a way to resolve this dilemma. The answer lies, I submit, in distinguishing capitalism as a socio-economic system from the scientific technology upon which it is based. If this distinction is borne in mind, the possibility emerges of a form of social criticism which preserves the traditional utopian aversion to the injustices promulgated in the name of capitalism, yet itself embraces those rational modes of thought which select among available choices the most efficient means of realizing projected ends. Thus we must distinguish carefully between the utopian's moral revulsion against the inequitable distribution of surplus value under capitalism and his attitude toward the plant and technology upon which that capitalist order is based. Hatred of the factory system need not be construed as hatred of the machines within its walls, nor construed to imply rejection of those forms of rationality which made the invention of the machine possible in the first place.

One further objection may rest upon a thoroughly Western assumption. The assumption is that the inevitable end product of modernization and rational planning must be a capitalist order. Following Ferdinand Tonnies's useful distinctions, it is further assumed that, wherever modernization takes place, *Gemein-*

schaft institutions must give way to *Gesellschaft* forms.[5] Utopianism, therefore, with its affinity for pre-modern communitarianism and its alleged regressive exultation of primary relationships, is dismissed by definition as an improbable contributor
to the development of an industrial society.

Japanese scholars have begun to object to the too-ready im-
position of Western definitions of modernization upon non-
Western nations.[6] Our plea for a reexamination of the role *Gemeinschaft* institutions may play in the process of modernization
in follower nations may be all the more crucial in the case of
Japan because of the ease with which she advanced toward modernity, the important role the traditional sector of the economy
played in providing capital for that forward leap, and the persistence of communalistic forms and relationships deep into modern times. Furthermore, the fact is that Japan's modernizing elite
frequently rejected Western capitalistic prototypes in favor of
institutions borrowed from the utopian socialist tradition. (The
Raiffeisen cooperatives and Danish Folk Higher Schools are two
examples that come readily to mind.) I suggest that, at least in
the Japanese context, there is no inherent reason why industrial
progress cannot be directed toward utopian, communalistic
goals, particularly if the projected future is infused with the
spirit of rational planning and regard for social controls.

I I I

So far I have been operating upon a premise of cultural diffusion.
Rational modes of utopian thought infused with the planning ele-

---

[5] Ferdinand Tonnies, *Community and Society* (New York: Harper &
Row, 1963), pp. 258–59.

[6] John W. Hall, "Changing Conceptions of the Modernization of
Japan," in Marius B. Jansen, ed., *Changing Japanese Attitudes toward
Modernization* (Princeton, N.J.: Princeton University Press, 1965), p. 38.

ment were borrowed from the West and injected into the Japanese context. But did social planning exist in Japan in some form prior to the appearance of Western utopianism during the Meiji period? I have not pushed my preliminary inquiry back beyond the restructuring of Japan by the Tokugawa household in 1603; however, I argue that a planning tradition did in fact grace the Tokugawa intellectual scene, and that it took its rise from a revived interest in the Neo-Confucian thought imported by Ieyasu to legitimate his new regime.

Viewed in this light, there are many aspects of Neo-Confucianism, both in its orthodox and heretical forms, that may have contributed to the emergence of a utopian planning tradition. To begin with, it has been observed that the utopian is a personality type unable to tolerate the existence of human imperfection or evil.[7] Much like the Neo-Confucian philosopher, he insists upon the innate goodness of man, visualizing an inner stock of virtue (in Neo-Confucian terminology, *te*) which has become defiled by life in an unclean world. Therefore, much like the Neo-Confucian *chün-tzu*, or sage, the utopian may orient his life toward the pursuit of personal perfection, a quest which when projected outward may take the form of a social mission to rejuvenate and cleanse his fellow man. As his mission unfolds, the utopian frequently holds before the masses the social idea of cosmic love (in Neo-Confucian parlance, *jen*) under the aegis of which harmony can be established between men, within an institutional context of primary *Gemeinschaft* relationships. Like the Neo-Confucian, he may argue that this is man's natural state because man himself stands between heaven and earth as an integral part of the eternal triad and is not divorced from the natural world as he seems to have become in the Western Judaeo-Christian tradition. Neo-Confucianism even provided potential

---

[7] Thomas Molnar, *Utopia, the Perennial Heresy* (New York: Sheed and Ward, 1967), pp. 4–8.

Japanese utopians with an ideal millennial age, though that golden era was lodged in a Chinese mythical past and in its strangeness did not particularly appeal to their mentality until it occurred to the Japanese scholars to recast their own Taika period in the mold of this Elysian paradise. During the mid-nineteenth century, the vista of this Taika millennium would in fact provide a symbolic focus for social reorganization at the time of the Meiji restoration.

In spite of these predisposing factors, I am reluctant to claim a truly utopian tradition for Japan prior to the Meiji period. This too must not be ruled out of hand, since the combination of this-worldly action and the prophetic vision of a pending golden age in Nichiren Buddhism comes to mind. But Nichiren Buddhism became the special object of hostility and repression on the part of the Tokugawa regime at the turn of the seventeenth century.[8] Hence, we are all the more forced to search for precedents within the borrowed Neo-Confucian tradition. As is well known, this philosophic system was highly rational, positivistic, and rigidly oriented in its orthodox form toward the exaltation of ethical, harmonious, human relationships. Moreover, the primary stress in orthodox Neo-Confucianism as propounded by Chu Hsi and his rival Wang Yang-ming was toward knowledge in action, and to this end both men enjoined their students to "investigate things."[9] The true import of this phrase is presently the subject of considerable controversy, but, nevertheless, what is important is the fact that Japanese intellectuals universally interpreted this phrase as a pragmatic injunction to analyze nature into its component parts. This empirical, analytical approach to nature,

[8] Masaharu Anesaki, *History of Japanese Religion, with Special Reference to the Social and Moral Life of the Nation* (Rutland, Vt., and Tokyo: Charles E. Tuttle Co., 1963), pp. 230–33.

[9] William T. deBary, ed., *Sources of Japanese Tradition* (New York: Columbia University Press, 1958), p. 351.

we believe, has had more than a little to do with the formation of that hard-headed, practical response of Japanese thinkers to Western learning following European impact. Indeed, this positive approach to nature and reality (*jitsugaku*) runs through the thought of the Tokugawa period and surfaces in a wide variety of practical proposals for reform at the time of the restoration in 1868.

But there are additional factors in Neo-Confucianism which tend to support our argument. Of interest in the light of Professor Diamond's investigation of the idea of the primitive[10] was the almost universal rejection on the part of Japanese intellectuals of the fundamental Neo-Confucian dualism between idea and objective reality. Much in the fashion of Plato, the great Sung philosopher, Chu Hsi, had surmised that each category of material substance was simply an objective manifestation of an underlying explanatory principle, *li*. Right from the outset our Japanese pre-utopians, many of them Zen priests, would have nothing to do with this dualism, preferring to transform it into a monistic existential life force, called *ki*, which they believed immanently transfused all earthly existence. This is as true of such orthodox Neo-Confucians as Itō Jinsai, Ogyū Sorai, and Miura Baien as of thinkers less Confucian in orientation such as Kaibara Ekken, Yamaga Sokō, or Ninomiya Sontoku.

Now this monistic, non-Platonic synthesis we find emerging in the early Tokugawa period is very important, for what I believe these nascent social engineers lacked to make their approach to the world dynamic and futuristic was a progressive and meliorizing view of time conceived as a unilinear progression through stages of development toward some ideal end. Neo-Confucianism had reawakened the Japanese intellectual's interest in historical

[10] Stanley Diamond, "The Search for the Primitive," in Ashley Montagu, ed., *The Concept of the Primitive* (New York: Free Press, 1968), esp. pp. 128–30.

process but provided him with only a cyclical construction of time which tended to direct his attention back toward an ideal past. There the Tokugawa scholar rediscovered and began to embellish the Japanese imperial tradition which, according to the newly recovered Shinto myths, stressed the unbroken descent of the emperor from Jimmu Tennō. Thus, long before the nineteenth-century Shinto revival which was to lead eventually to a virulent pre-restoration nationalism, men like Itō Jinsai (1627–1705) had begun to stress the dynamism of a universe suffused with the all-powerful life force *ki* and, in keeping with this organismic world view, commenced to apply this idea of progress to the realm of human affairs.[11] Expanding upon this theme, Itō's student, Ogyū Sorai (1666–1727), emphasized that the *tao* ("way of man") must harmonize with the laws of natural change.[12] Moreover, building upon this idea, Ogyū appears to have been the first to suggest that the true sage is a man who takes thought for the future and seeks to plan social reforms to prevent contingencies from disturbing the institutional order.[13]

Miura Baien (1723–89), a Neo-Confucian steeped in this organismic developmental tradition, went one step beyond Ogyū with his very Hegelian interpretation of change as the product of the dialectical interaction of natural forces.[14] At the same time, Miura was an unorthodox skeptic and rationalist par excellence who wrote ponderous treatises on economics which included cooperative schemes for rural village reform.[15] But perhaps no pre-restoration figure fits this pattern of social engineer as does Nino-

[11] Joseph J. Spae, *Itō Jinsai, a Philosopher, Educator, and Sinologist of the Tokugawa Period* (New York: Paragon Book Reprint Corp., 1967), pp. 101–3; deBary, *Sources of Japanese Tradition*, p. 411.

[12] J. R. McEwan, *The Political Writings of Ogyū Sorai* (Cambridge: Cambridge University Press, 1962), pp. 7, 10, 11.

[13] Ibid., p. 30.

[14] de Bary, *Sources of Japanese Tradition*, pp. 491–92.

[15] Ibid., p. 489.

miya Sontoku (1787–1856), whose stress upon the importance of agrarian planning and whose devotion to the ideal of cooperative self-help served as a model for many utopian visionaries during the Meiji and Taisho periods.

IV

In the immediate post-restoration period in Japan, we still find no social phenomena we could confidently label utopian. However, we witness the growth and amplification of the tradition of social planning we have traced forward from the beginning of the Tokugawa era. Since Meiji was an age of public service, during which many young men aspired to positions in the new bureaucracy, it is not surprising to find the idea of planning carried forward largely by men in the higher echelons of government who had successfully made the transition from samurai to modern bureaucrat. Prominent in this regard were the members of the *Meirokusha* (Meiji Six Society), all of whom played leading roles in the introduction of Western ideas. Among these, for example, Nishi Amane had been deeply influenced during youth by the teachings of Ogyū Sorai. Nishi, in keeping with the *jitsugaku* tradition, was instrumental in spreading the positivistic doctrines of Auguste Comte and the utilitarian beliefs of John Stuart Mill in Meiji intellectual circles.[16] In the realm of communalistic ideals, Mori Arinori, also a member of the *Meirokusha* and later Minister of Education, exhibited an abiding interest in the Harris brotherhood during his visit to the United States in 1867.[17]

[16] Thomas R. H. Havens, "Comte, Mill, and the Thought of Nishi Amane in Meiji Japan," *Journal of Asian Studies* 27 (1968):217–28.

[17] Herbert Passin, *Society and Education in Japan* (New York: Columbia University Press, 1965), p. 90.

Another member of the society, Nakamura Masanao, was instrumental in translating Smiles's *Self Help* into Japanese.[18]

A relatively unstudied but promising rival society of young intellectuals called themselves the *Kyōsan Dōshū* (Cooperative Community) and pledged to work for social reform based upon cooperative ideals.[19] As in the case of the *Meirokusha*, many of these stalwarts, among them Baba Tatsui, Yano Fumio, and Kaneko Kentarō, came forward to assume leading roles in the Meiji reform movement. Further evidence of the importance of cooperative planning principles during this time may be seen in *Kōgyō Iken,* that long-range plan for economic achievement drawn up in 1884 by the Ministry of Agriculture and Commerce, stressing the spirit of practical self-help as the guiding ideal of the Meiji government's deflationary modernization program.[20] Curiously enough, Shinagawa Yajirō, who later as Home Minister was instrumental in introducing the Raiffeisen cooperative movement into Japan, was a member of this planning commission. Furthermore, as an avid disciple of Ninomiya Sontoku, Shinagawa was also an impassioned advocate of the *Hōtokusha* movement during the 1880's as the means to remedy the economic ills of rural Japan.[21] The whole subject is greatly in need of study, but perhaps this is sufficient to indicate the intense interest among Meiji officialdom both in native and foreign forms of communalism, as well as their readiness to apply the principles of communitarian planning to the affairs of state.

[18] Anesaki, *History of Japanese Religion,* p. 353.

[19] Ibid., pp. 350–53.

[20] See Ichirou Inukai, "Kōgyō Iken, the World's First Attempt at Planning Economic Development" (Manuscript, The Japan-Korean Studies Center Colloquim, University of California at Berkeley, 1965).

[21] Kawade Takeo, ed., *Nihon rekishi daijiten,* vol. 9 (Tokyo: Kawade Shobō, 1956–60), p. 295.

V

It appears incontestable that the outcropping of utopian movements on the eve of the Russo-Japanese War reflected the strains induced by Japan's first serious efforts at full-scale modernization. What is not so clear is whether these movements were influenced by the historical factors discussed above, were indicative of the diffusion of utopianism from abroad, or actually constituted something *sui generis* on the Japanese social scene. Recall that at that time the first generation of Meiji youth completely socialized under the new national school system was coming of age, and that only recently they had been exposed to a curriculum revision which liberally doused them with doctrines of *Nihon-shugi* and a virulent nationalism. To escape the ennui of *kokutai,* they fled into the works of the Christian anarchist Tolstoy, the nihilism of Nietzsche, or turned to embrace reviving Nichiren Buddhism. The result was something of a value crisis for late Meiji youth. Intense egoism, flight into religious mysticism, bohemian indulgences, and sometimes pathetic surrender in suicide became the fashion of the day.[22] If it were our purpose to develop a morphology of utopianism for modern Japan, there is little doubt that the first decade of the twentieth century would constitute its prophetic and heroic phase.

But here we are concerned with rational forms of utopianism, and it is, therefore, instructive that it was in this period, too, that Fabianism, a genre of utopian socialism that rigorously embraced the ideal of social planning, was introduced from abroad by liberal American clergymen to a small socialist study group meeting in the Unitarian Church in Tokyo.[23] Representing as it

[22] Anesaki, *History of Japanese Religion,* pp. 375–77.
[23] Hyman Kublin, *Asian Revolutionary: The Life of Sen Katayama* (Princeton, N.J.: Princeton University Press, 1964), p. 133.

did the futuristic schemes for social reform of the best minds in
Britain (Shaw, the Webbs, MacDonald, Pease, Hobson, Wallas,
and many others), Fabian doctrines could not but leave a deep
impression upon the minds of the founders of the Japanese socialist movement. Under the influence of this form of social engineering, Suzuki Bunji and Abe Isō were instrumental in organizing early socialist study groups in Tokyo, the most important
of which was the *Yūaikai* (Friendly Society) founded in 1912
upon the principles of British craft unionism, Christian harmon-
ism, and mutual aid.[24]

The era of readjustment in Britain following World War I
witnessed the gradual extinction of those rational utopian socialist ideals that had guided the English industrial union movement during the European conflict. In Japan, however, where
guild socialism had taken root among urban and rural workers
newly awakening to political self-consciousness, such sentiments
did not die. To the contrary, through the untiring efforts of Kagawa Toyohiko, Sugiyama Motojirō, Murashima Yoriyuki, and
other energetic young Christian socialists, guild ideals found expression in a host of political, social, and religious movements.
The most important of these following the great Kawasaki dock-
yard strike was the farm-tenant movement organized by liberal
Japanese Christians in 1922.[25] To counter the irrational militancy
of the anarcho-syndicalists then sweeping the industrial unions,
Kagawa routinized guild-utopian idealism into the charter of the
tenant farmers' newly organized Japan Farmers' Union.[26] Moreover, it was his idea to employ from that Western, rational, utopian tradition he so admired the rationale of Christian coopera-

[24] Ibid., p. 223.
[25] Sumiya Mikio, *Kagawa Toyohiko, jin to shisō shiriizu* (Tokyo:
Nihon Kirisuto Kyōdan Shuppanbu, 1960), p. 135.
[26] Yokoyama Haruichi, *Kagawa Toyohiko den* (Tokyo: Kirisuto
Shimbunsha, 1950), p. 184.

tivism in order to bind together the rural and urban proletarian leagues and lay the institutional foundation for a new, communal, economic order.[27] However, by 1924, communist penetration rendered all utopian planning of this sort nugatory, and neither the badly fragmented industrial union movement nor the then-nucleating proletarian party movement appeared to Kagawa to offer a suitable alternative for the prosecution of his utopian socialist purposes.

This quandary was resolved by the great Tokyo earthquake of 1923. It reduced the nation's capital to rubble, engendering in the minds of the masses a sense of shock and malaise unequaled in psychological impact since the death of the Meiji emperor. Perhaps, as Maruyama has suggested,[28] the new and modern city which arose out of the ashes of the quake symbolized graphically for the common man the irrevocable passing of traditional society and the transforming power of mechanization. Significantly for our purposes, the post-quake adjustment period saw the wholesale importation of the accoutrements of urban capitalism into the capital city, in response to which a host of messianic and chiliastic movements mushroomed in the Kantō region. Some of these, like *Reiyūkai*, religious in tone, traced their origins back to the romantic period of Japanese utopianism at the time of the Russo-Japanese War. Others, like *Sekai Kyūseikyō* and *Seichō no Ie*, movements messianic and salvationist in tone founded by businessmen ruined by the earthquake and fire, arose in direct response to the horrors of the Kantō disaster itself.[29] Thus, what-

[27] Takeda-Cho Kiyo, "An Essay on Kagawa Toyohiko, the Place of Man in His Social Theory," *Ajia Bunka Kenkyū* 2 (1960):47–68.

[28] Masao Maruyama, "Patterns of Individuation and the Case of Japan: A Conceptual Scheme," in Marius B. Jansen, ed., *Changing Japanese Attitudes toward Modernization* (Princeton, N.J.: Princeton University Press, 1965), esp. p. 517.

[29] Clark B. Offner and Henry Van Straelen, *Modern Japanese Religions, with Special Emphasis upon Their Doctrines of Healing* (New York: Twayne Publishers, 1963), pp. 73, 78.

ever the significance of the Tokyo quake for the broader perspective of Japanese history, there is little doubt that the natural disturbances of 1923 were of signal importance for the development of Japan's utopian movements.

But we are concerned with rational forms of utopianism, and while marking the messianic and eschatological character of utopian-related religions in the post-earthquake period, it is to those sacerdotal undertakings more Christian in inspiration that we must turn for further evidence for our theme. While the quake revealed the gross inadequacies of Buddhist-related movements in the realm of disaster relief and social services, many Japanese Christian denominations seized the opportunity to display their public-spiritedness, and through their relief missions they earned the gratitude and admiration of the Yamamoto cabinet. Scarcely had the echoes from these plaudits died when the Christians launched a national evangelical crusade which was designed to take the message of the social gospel into every hamlet.[30] The professed goal of this ecumenical quest for one million souls for Christ was to establish the Kingdom of God on earth, an end such Tolstoyan utopians as Nishida Tenkō, Arishima Takeo, and Mushakōji Saneatsu could well comprehend.[31] Nevertheless, upon closer inspection we see that, rather than the vague encomiums of Christian anarchism, the institutional prospectus of this evangelical gospel crusade was nothing less than Western cooperativism and guild industrial unionism thinly veiled in orthodox theological dressing.

The Kingdom of God movement flourished, despite the economic chaos attendant upon Black Friday, largely through the herculean efforts of its leader, Kagawa, and his self-effacing assistant, Kuroda Shirō. But, curiously, the world depression which began to hit Japan hard by 1931 did not trumpet forth the pro-

---

[30] Yokoyama, *Kagawa Toyohiko den*, pp. 287–98, 315–34.
[31] Anesaki, *History of Japanese Religion*, pp. 400–403.

fusion of utopian-related movements in response to the jarring economic dislocations of these years that we might have come to expect. One can only speculate on the possible reasons for this: overemphasis upon the tensions induced by the depression, the existence of alternate channels for emotional release, the vicarious and diverting psychological effect of the Manchurian venture, military conscription of potential folk leaders, and so forth. Still, though utopian movements did not arise *de novo* at this time, we cannot overlook the widespread appeal of Christian messianism with its stress upon personal salvation and promise of earthly rewards in a not too distant future, especially in rural Japan. These eschatological propensities can be observed in many of the "quake-born" folk religions as well, for both *Ōmotokyō* and *Seichō no Ie* preached the momentary impendence of a new and splendid age.[32] Moreover, such utopian perspectives were a feature, too, of the Nichiren-related religions which had the highly eschatological Buddhist tradition of *mappō* upon which to draw.[33] One could toy around with the question of influences of one movement upon the other and miss altogether the broader and more important question of how to explain the presence of this utopian intendment in the ethos of these quasi-religions at this particular juncture in history.

Not the depression low but the years 1934–36 were crucial for the viability of these various messianic causes. The Kingdom of God movement, for example, was dissolved by mutual agreement of its members in 1934. However, the various credit, marketing, producer, and consumer cooperatives which the movement spawned lived on, and, indeed, the Peasant Gospel School movement patterned by Sugiyama Motojirō and Kagawa Toyo-

[32] Offner and Van Straelen, *Modern Japanese Religions*, pp. 70, 79.
[33] Horace N. McFarland, *The Rush Hour of the Gods: A Study of New Religious Movements in Japan* (New York: Macmillan, 1967), p. 202.

hiko after the Folk Higher Schools of Denmark flourished and
spread throughout Japan.[34] But understandably, any deeply utopian movements, particularly those which espoused a radical
political program, would sooner or later earn the enmity of an increasingly Fascist regime. It is, therefore, difficult to escape the
conclusion that the death of liberal democracy was decisive for
all utopian-oriented movements during the early 1930's, both
those rational and chiliastic in nature. Not only did the Kingdom
of God movement pass from view in 1934, but in that year the
schism occurred which brought forth *Sekai Kyūseikyō* with its
universalistic world salvation program. The second *Ōmotokyō*
incident occurred in 1935, and from this time forward even *Hito
no Michi* and those sects attempting to accommodate to ultra-
nationalism by the incorporation of *kokutai* doctrines into their
theology came under government persecution. The profundity
of this official suspicion of utopian-tinged movements becomes
all the more apparent when we consider the inability of such
grass-root Fascist organizations as those fostered by Tachibana
Kōsaburō and Gondō Seikyō, with their communitarian view
of the future, to survive the rise of the military to power.

The underlying reason for this enduring hostility on the part
of the Japanese government toward all utopian movements is not
far to seek, for it is perfectly clear that almost all such communalistic utopian sects either implicitly or explicitly threatened that
capitalistic economic substructure with which military Fascism
had decided to compromise. Therefore, utopian-socialist and
Christian-anarchist perspectives of days to come, however misty
and vague in conception, could not be tolerated by a government whose own vista of the future à la New Order in East
Asia would be founded upon colonialism and monopoly capitalism. Thus, in contrast to the typical utopian's concern to trans-

[34] Yokoyama, *Kagawa Toyohiko den*, pp. 263–67.

cend the present, Japanese Fascism chose its prototypes from an imperialist West of four decades past, and so, dedicated to the maintenance and preservation of *zaibatsu* capitalism, found it impossible to tolerate the implied transiliency of all futuristic religious and social movements oriented toward communitarian reforms.

VI

The freedoms guaranteed by Japan's post-war constitution have encouraged the reemergence of utopian idealism into full flower, and today a wide variety of communalistic movements in one way or another proclaim the virtues of Japan reborn.[35] Although the programs of these sects are highly eclectic, and few afford evidence of that serious attention to long-range means-ends planning which has been the focus of this essay, most of them share a vision of the future in which the human personality will undergo some form of spiritual regeneration as the condition precedent to a terminal age of love, peace, and brotherhood. Thus in post-war Japan we witness a revival of that messianism and acosmism which infused the thinking of the religious utopians during the 1930's. This trend toward universalism and internationalism now evident in Japan has deeply affected the pre-war tradition of social planning. On the one hand, those future-oriented sects which do profess to plan appear to be extraordinarily vague concerning the institutional structure of their heralded tomorrows. Yet, on the other hand, it seems to this writer that today many more movements have become captivated by the blue-printing spirit of pre-war utopian socialism. And so, paradoxically, at a time when the utopian socialist cause is dying

[35] David W. Plath, "The Fate of Utopia: Adaptive Tactics in Four Japanese Groups," *American Anthropologist* 68 (1966):1152–61.

out in Japan, many new, pure, and quasi-utopian–oriented movements exhibit a moderate concern for internal rationalization and futuristic means-ends planning. We leave to contemporary investigators the task of evaluating the contribution this revived interest in planning may have made to the present economic boom. More important, it remains to be seen whether such enormously successful quasi-utopian organizations as Sōka Gakkai will ever go beyond mere opportunism and awake to the moral responsibilities long-range planning of this sort demands.[36] In my opinion, the long-term purposive action required for the successful proselytization of any utopian movement cannot be sustained except in terms of values with ultimate appeal. Thus it will be interesting to see whether any of the utopian-oriented groups which now dot the Japanese social scene will be able to survive without eventually couching their reform goals in terms of some transcendental frame of reference.

VII

In summary, I have suggested that, since the turn of the twentieth century, utopianism has seldom earned its Marxian label of medieval retreatism. On the contrary, modern forms of utopianism incorporate an element of rational planning which may make an important contribution to the process of modernization. This is especially true in non-Western follower nations where there is no particular reason to assume that the end product of the industrializing process must be capitalism. Something of the sort seems to have been true of Japan, where rational forms of utopianism introduced from abroad helped to assuage the imbalance

[36] Robert N. Bellah, ed., *Religion and Progress in Modern Asia* (New York: Free Press, 1965), pp. 195, 214.

caused by rapid modernization through its effective routinization into a wide variety of social reform movements.

However, Japan may have been unique in that this imported utopian tradition did not fall upon deaf ears. Rather, the Japanese appear to have evolved an indigenous communitarian planning tradition during the Tokugawa period, the spirit of which was carried forward into modern times by enlightened Meiji bureaucrats. This tradition was seized upon by utopians at the time of the Russo-Japanese War and successfully synthesized with Fabian and guild socialist doctrines to present the working proletariat a blueprint of the future which would contain the fruits of modernization, though rationally reallocated under the aegis of collective controls. Utopian socialists interjected this view of the future into the labor movement, the farm-tenant movement, the cooperative movement, the social gospel movement, and a host of lesser causes. Weathering in this guise the labor turmoil of World War I, the psychological impact of the great Tokyo quake, and the economic dislocations of the depression, such rational modes of utopianism witnessed the emergence of a plethora of secular and quasi-religious imitators before eventually succumbing to emergent military Fascism during the 1930's.

In post–World War II Japan, utopian socialism, the standard-bearer of this rational utopian tradition, is on the wane; it is still far from clear whether the multiplicity of future-oriented sects and associations which have mushroomed in the more liberal post-war atmosphere will utilize the spirit of planning for long-range social purposes. If something of the sort should be the case, especially if a concern arises to see that ethical means be fitted to transcendent universalistic ends, it is possible that Japanese utopianism may make its greatest contribution to modernization in the post-war period.

3. *Political Futuristics: Toward the Study of Alternative Political Futures*

JAMES ALLEN DATOR
University of Hawaii

In this brief paper, I wish to indicate what I mean by "political futuristics" and to show how it fits into the scientific study of politics and relates to the investigation of utopia from modern viewpoints.

I do not wish to trace here the development of political science from its predominantly Greek beginnings to the present. I intend instead to start with some of the sources which were most strongly felt when an academic discipline called political science was first formed at the end of the nineteenth and beginning of the twentieth centuries. In addition, I will be concerned primarily with political science in America rather than throughout the world.

American political science may be regarded as having been formed by the splitting off of the politically concerned branches of three older disciplines—history, philosophy, and law[1]—and the tenuous grafting together of these three into a common discipline which continued to emphasize the preoccupations of these three sources, and which failed to develop a common theoretical root out of them or from any other source. With some outstanding but very rare exceptions,[2] until the end of World War II, American political science, in its teaching and research, could be characterized as being essentially the descriptive history of certain formal political institutions of the United States, England, Germany, and France; the historical and sometimes normative consideration of certain Western philosophers (from the Greeks to St. Thomas, to Locke and Hobbes, and to the Founding Fathers, seldom further); and the study of the (mainly)written constitutions, legislative enactments, and judicial decisions of the four countries named above.

Even though it may be reducing this description of the development of the discipline somewhat to a caricature, I will assert that, because of the narrowness and sterility of these foci, American political science underwent a crisis and subsequent partial transformation during and just after World War II. It became evident that the profession could offer little in the way of practical yet scientifically tested advice to policy-makers when the American government was faced with the problem of reorganiz-

[1] Political science also owes a considerable debt to economics; but this discipline, too, was in the process of formation at about the same time that political science was.

[2] For example, Charles Merriam, Harold Gosnell, and Harold Lasswell pioneered in behavioral and statistical work in the 1920's and 1930's at the University of Chicago, and there was here and there an occasional student of exotic Western or non-Western politics.

ing the political systems of occupied countries in Europe and Asia. The focus of American political science was so overwhelmingly Anglo-American, legalistic, historical, and anecdotal that little other than the recitation of the principles and institutions of the American federal government could be given by American political scientists in reply to such questions as, "How can democratic governments, supported by democratic citizens, be achieved in countries which have not developed them on their own?" American policy-makers discovered that it was seldom political scientists, but more frequently the anthropologists, sociologists, and social psychologists, who were able to offer seemingly more convincing answers to their questions. At least, it became evident, these disciplines were concerned with human behavior and the relationship between human institutions and human behavior. Moreover, though admittedly far from being fully integrated themselves and not possessing a completely satisfactory methodology or theory for the solution of their problems, still anthropology, sociology, and social psychology did seem to be more on the right road than did most American political science. Thus (to omit a great deal of what actually did happen), American political science came to have injected into it the methods and theories of these behavioral disciplines, and there has developed in political science an increasingly vigorous stream of behaviorally oriented scholarship.[3]

At the same time, and equally a part of this, was the introduction of two "tool" disciplines into political science. The first, both chronologically and in terms of current total impact, is statistics, and the second is mathematics.

Statistics is needed to provide a way of describing or categoriz-

---

[3] David Easton has conveniently summarized the essence of the behavioral approach in his article, "The Current Meaning of 'Behavioralism,'" in James C. Charlesworth, ed., *Contemporary Political Analysis* (New York: Free Press, 1967), pp. 16ff.

ing the vast amounts of quantitative data which behavioral methods are collecting. Even more important (in conjunction with a growing interest in rigorous, theoretically informed, and testable research designs, in contrast to the more episodical and intuitive methods of the traditional approaches), statistics provides methods of testing hypotheses from behavioral data and thus helps make possible an inductive and empirical political *science*.

More recently, some American political scientists have grown dissatisfied with primarily inductive methods and have pointed out that since even seemingly pure inductive and empirical political scientists apparently have a prior (and deductive) model in their heads of what politics is, what a political "fact" is, and how these political facts might relate together in order to be tested empirically, it is imperative that we pay more attention to the construction of these deductive models. Since a major requirement of such a model is that it be rigorously, logically, and unambiguously stated (and yet that it be framed in such a way that it can be empirically tested at some point), many political scientists are turning to mathematics for aid in constructing models which meet these criteria.[4]

It would be quite erroneous to allege, in terms of research output, but especially in terms of classroom content and study, that American political science today is dominated by its behavioral/

---

[4] For example, Kenneth Arrow, *Social Choice and Individual Values* (New York: Wiley, 1951); Paul Lazarsfeld, ed., *Mathematical Thinking in the Social Sciences* (New York: Free Press, 1954); Anthony Downs, *An Economic Theory of Democracy* (New York: Harper, 1957); R. Duncan Luce and Howard Raffia, *Games and Decisions* (New York: Wiley, 1958); Duncan Black, *The Theory of Committees and Elections* (Cambridge: Cambridge University Press, 1958); James Buchanan and Gordon Tullock, *The Calculus of Consent* (Ann Arbor: University of Michigan Press, 1962); William Riker, *The Theory of Politican Coalitions* (New Haven: Yale University Press, 1963); Hayward Alker, Jr., *Mathematics and Politics* (New York: Macmillan, 1965); Gordon Tullock, *Toward a Mathematics of Politics* (Ann Arbor: University of Michigan Press, 1967).

statistical/mathematical branches. A great deal of American political science remains institutional, legalistic, and historical; in short, a great deal of American political science is concerned only with certain aspects of *the past*. In a way, American political science can be viewed as a profession at war with itself over methodology, with the victory of the newer approaches by no means assured.

Yet it is our major interest here not to determine who is winning or who will win, but rather to point out that while the behavioral approaches have made a considerable impact on American political science and have gone a long way toward making political science a more *useful* science, still the great majority of even the behavioral studies, while perhaps rigorous in research design and hypothesis testing, tend to be studies only of the *recent past*. That is, while considerable concern has been given to data identification, collection, and analysis, and to the theory underlying such procedures, still, when the last chapter in the book or the last paragraph in the article is written, where the researcher tries to tell what the future holds in store for the object of his research, the writer generally falls back on his intuitive resources. Out goes the rigor and the theory; in comes the hunch and the guess. We may be sufficiently impressed by the data collection and analysis to be willing to believe the guess, but we certainly lay aside, and in a significant way render ludicrous, our earlier insistence on rigor. Should we not be equally concerned with the development of methodologies and theories for the study of the future? Should we not be equally concerned with the basis of our conjectures about how the phenomenon under study will turn out? If we reject the imprecision and intuition of the traditional inside-dopester and descriptive storyteller of political ancedotes, should we not also be wary of the behaviorist who projects the future on the same thin thread of intuitive fancy?

The measure of any science, it seems to me, is how well it *explains, predicts,* and *controls* the phenomena of interest. Many of the natural sciences can explain and predict quite well; some can control. Political science can do none of these. Yet, I believe, to the extent that it seeks to be a science, political science should aim for these three goals. To do this, political science must be concerned with developing methodologies which take account of the future as well as of the past and the present.

The rise of the digital and analog computers has done much to speed the use of behavioral and statistical methods in political science. Indeed, most political science utilization of computers has been as high-speed calculators of mountains of data.

Yet probably the most important imminent use of the computer is in the area of simulation rather than data analysis. The speed and memory of the computer makes it possible to simulate infinitely variable socio-political situations and systems. Thus the computer facilitates the design and study—and achievement or prevention—of a great variety of alternative futures. Along with methods and techniques appropriate for this endeavor—set theory, matrix algebra, linear programming, Markov chains, game theory, linear and non-linear trend analysis, and the like—the computer makes futuristics possible. That is to say, the design and analysis of alternative futures, and the development of theories and methodologies for the study of these futures, is now possible and, I think, imperative.

At a time when we were technologically and conceptually unable to study, plan for, and guide the future, we could perhaps justify our lack of scholarly concern for it. We could leave to writers of utopian novels and science fiction, and to religious and political visionaries, the dream of a better—or worse—life to come. But I believe we are beginning to understand that our images of the past, present, and future, our present acts or refusals to act, and the occurence of expected or unexpected future events will shape that life to come. The future does not "just happen," but is determined in large measure by us in the present; we can shape the future to be more nearly the way we want it to be. If so, then we must take seriously the necessity of determining the type of future we want and work for its actualization. See how the "traditional" concern of normative political philosophy —determining the "good society"—returns as the central question of political futuristics!

It is my contention, then, that this new potentiality and new responsibility will have an impact even more revolutionary for the political science profession than was that of the earlier introduction of behavioral and statistical methods. However, just as there are many different methods, theories, and interests contained in the phrase, "the behavioral approach to political science," so also I believe that political futuristics will have a many-faceted thrust. So far, I see four mainstreams:

1. Using tools (especially the computer) and techniques (such as linear programming) similar to those of the technological and market forecaster, political futuristics may mean *the forecasting of the evolutionary change of socio-political institutions, attitudes, and behavior.* It should be clear that I do not mean here the prediction of political events, like the victor in a presidential election, but the forecasting of (possible or expected) changes in the socio-political system itself. Further, I have in mind here the simple, linear projection of gradual modifications of existing institutions (etc.) according to present trends, without the forecaster, as such, being interested in achieving or modifying these trends, and without considering the conscious or accidental introduction of new, currently non-existent or unimagined factors.

2. Political futuristics may be *the construction of "what if" computer-assisted models of the future.* Here, in the manner of some foreign and military policy planners (RAND Corporation, Hudson Institute), the futurist is interested in determining the

possible and/or likely consequences of the introduction of new factors into a real or imagined socio-political system. What would be the consequences if, holding everything else constant, we abolished the present method of nominating and electing the president and vice-president, and did it all by direct popular participation, through the medium of a central computer with remote access terminals in every home? What would be the consequences on our present socio-political system if the average life span were suddenly trebled? What would be the effect of abolishing the current court system and replacing it with a self-service, computer-based adjudicative system?

3. Political futuristics may mean *the design and operation of complete future (utopian or non-utopian) socio-political systems.* This could take the form of pure computer simulations; man-computer simulations; board games (à la Monopoly); man-man, non-realtime simulations (à la mock United Nations, scenarioed plays, socio-drama, etc.); or—in the manner of typical utopian communities—man-man, realtime simulations.[5]

4. Political futuristics may take the form of *the controlled, systematic projection by groups of experts of what selected aspects of the future might be like* (for example, as in the Delphi technique), *or single-person, more or less random and unsystematic estimations of future socio-political developments* informed by a reading of and reflection on the literature of science fiction, technological developments, military forecasting, scientific and medical innovations, and the like. I wish to make it clear that I am not in any way disparaging this last approach. The introduction of such a modest futuristic concern into traditional behav-

[5] For a brief, interesting example of some of these, see Arthur Waskow, "Looking Forward: 1999," *New University Thought* 6 (1968):34–55; see also my research note, "Non-Verbal, Non-Numerical Models and Media in Political Science," *American Behavioral Scientist* 11 (1968): 9–11.

ioral research and teaching would be a great step forward. What progress to have American government courses taught not on the assumption that ours is a finished, eternally and everywhere valid and perfect political system whose attributes must be learned and worshipped, but rather that our governmental system must, if it is to be effective, adapt to (and indeed, anticipate and guide) changing conditions!

There very well may be other concerns which could properly be considered futuristic, but I believe these four are sufficiently inclusive to cover most of the field.

It seems clear to me, then, that whichever of the four forms it might take, some sort of serious concern for the future is imperative for political science—and indeed for all areas of scholarly concern. More traditional forms of futuristic attempts— literary utopias, small utopian communities, mass utopian sociopolitical movements—will of course continue to have their place. But they are, after all, only a restricted sample of the now richly varied futuristic possibilities which modern technology actualizes and, indeed, makes necessary.

I wish to encourage more scholars to turn their attention to the development of theories and methodologies for studying the future, and to make futuristic concerns an integral and obvious part of their teaching and research.

Recently, I heard an academician begin a question in a public meeting with the observation, "Of course, scholarship is the study of the past, but. . . ." Yes, scholarship is, too, the study of the past, but even more important, it seems to me, it is the study of the future.

 PART TWO

Utopian Strivings

INTRODUCTION

A. L. Kroeber once remarked that "any fool could devise a more consistent system than exists, but even a despot rarely can institute one."[1] Kroeber's quip can serve as a capsule summary of the difficulties any man has in translating his utopian vision into actuality. For he cannot in fact, as in fantasy, begin his work with untarnished men and untouched soil; he must build with those at hand. He must leap into the midst of that arena of conflict and discord that we call ordinary life.

Utopian image-work does not automatically unlock impulses to action. Often enough the utopigrapher himself is content to describe his otherland, and he does not furnish directions for getting there or bolster men's willingness to try. In order to move men, one must also create roles for them to play, dramas of suffering and salvation in which they may star; and one must coordinate their per-

[1] Alfred L. Kroeber, *The Nature of Culture* (Chicago: University of Chicago Press, 1952), p. 130.

formances. Visions, plans, and motivations are all three necessary for effective group action. It is an unusual individual who has talents of all three kinds—as prophet, planner, and leader.

In commonplace conversation, a utopian movement is one that creates collective settlements—the kibbutzim, for instance. For some groups, the commune is the ideal human living unit; for others, it is mainly a "testing station" (*jikkenchi*, the term favored by Japan's Yamagists). But many if not the majority of groups end up in little communes for other reasons. They may be determined to begin the new world here and now, even with a mere handful of workers, for example. Or they may reject violent overthrow (either on principle or as a matter of tactics), and so they must move to the edge of the vision-field scanned by local guardians of morality, in order to gain room to try the unconventional. Conversely, communes are a central tenet in some religious sects, such as the Hutterians; they too strive for otherworlds of a sort, but ones that could never be found in human life.

In Part One, we were attempting to enlarge the concept of utopia so as to cover more than imaginary island otherworlds à la Thomas More. In Part Two, we are attempting to enlarge the concept of utopian movements, or utopian activism, so as to cover more than commune socialism. Can we use some such concept to analyze the transcending-transforming aspects of collective action without diluting it into a nebulous notion of ultra-visionary striving? Joseph Gusfield takes up some of the difficulties this poses for the theorist. Harold Gould and Joseph L. Love pursue possible utopian elements in case studies of collective action during the Indian "mutiny" of the 1850's and among groups of Latin Americans. Finally, George L. Hicks shows how members of an "intentional community" in the United States have been able to sustain their utopian faith, even though their movement itself has virtually halted.

Gusfield starts from Karl Mannheim's distinction between ideology as a set of ideas for excusing the status quo and utopia as a set of ideas that justify transforming it. But, as Gusfield insists, global categorizations of this sort are too general to serve as an adequate frame for empirical analysis. We need concepts and patterns limited enough in scope so that they do not blot out the uniqueness of phenomena, yet broad enough to allow us to link cases from diverse epochs and continents. Mid-ground theories of this nature continue to be scarce in nearly all domains of social science. I am neither surprised nor discouraged by the fact that our brief conference failed to transcend this fundamental issue of comparative study in one glorious burst of dynamic group-think.

There are, as Gusfield points out, a host of typologies for social movements and collective action. I will draw upon these to suggest some features of utopian activism that invite investigation. These features seem to me to be common in utopianism, but possibly not unique to it. They may turn out to be distinctive of it, or they may not; this should be tested in controlled comparisons and contrasts of empirical cases.

Some typologies are concerned with *what* a movement seeks to change—e.g., Neil Smelser's distinction between norm-oriented and value-oriented activism. I find utopian striving hard to characterize in this way. In general it aims at "total" or at least pervasive social transformation. However, "Today Germany, tomorrow the world" has analogs in the rhetoric of many movements. We must learn to distinguish between when images of world change are meant as statements of actual plans and when they are meant primarily as motivational prods.

Other typologies deal with *how* the transformation is to be done —e.g., revolution verses reform. In this regard, Gusfield finds utopian striving especially interesting, since it so often seeks revolution by peaceful or non-political means. The utopian activist has to make do with the individual human stuff as it is, corrupted by local enculturation (though biotechnics offers intriguing new possibilities via transplants and cyborgs). He usually will, of course, pour great s into child training and into restructuring adult personalities me form of brainwashing. But if he cannot bypass soiled individuals, much as he may wish to, he can hope to bypass soiled institutions. Indeed, he may argue that institutions *must* be bypassed, lest they inevitably drag people back into the political muck. This adds to the impulse to found a little community in an out-of-the-way site. But as Gusfield indicates, it also aggravates the problem of managing tensions between one's commitment to apolitical means and one's need to compromise with local authority.[2]

We might, then, in a first approximation, sort out utopian, rebellious, and revolutionary activism according to whether they strive for change via persons or institutions. Rebellion would keep the institutions but have them run by better people; revolution would keep the people but give them better institutions. Utopianism would demand transformation both in persons and in institutions.

Still other typologies deal with *where* a movement wants to go— e.g., acculturative change patterned after an existing outland, or nativistic change patterned after a once-and-future way of life. By contrast with both of these, utopian striving is toward, in Anthony F. C. Wallace's phrasing, "a desired cultural end-state which has never been enjoyed by ancestors or foreigners."[3] Bruce P. Dohrenwend and Robert J. Smith make a similar contrast. Utopian movements, they say, "have not aimed to revive a Golden Age, nor do they profess to incorporate the essentials of any alien system. Theirs is a vision of the future and its pristine quality recommends it chiefly."[4]

On this score, utopian activism is more creative, unpredictable,

[2] See also my essay, "The Fate of Utopia: Adaptive Tactics in Four Japanese Groups," *American Anthropologist* 68 (1966):1152–62.
[3] Anthony F. C. Wallace, "Revitalization Movements," *American Anthropologist* 58 (1956):264–81.
[4] Bruce P. Dohrenwend and Robert J. Smith, "Toward a Theory of Acculturation," *Southwestern Journal of Anthropology* 18 (1962):30–39.

and emergent than other forms. The emergent properties of social action have been embarrassing to the social scientist with a vested interest in determinism. Numerous students have sketched abstract trajectories for the course of an ideal-typical social movement, in one or another set of stages from inspiration to institutionalization. These trajectories are helpful, but unilinear; social movements have a nasty tendency to skip stages, regress, or go off in still other directions.

Part of the difficulty is that emergent properties get masked by the metaphoric nature of symbols and actions. This compounds the social science task of trying to comprehend behavior from subjective as well as objective points of view. Men say one thing, mean another. They use old symbols to convey new ideas they sense but are unable to articulate. When Congressman Adam Clayton Powell, for instance, speaks of "getting this country back where it used to be"—I've heard him use the phrase—I doubt that he means to restore black slavery in the United States. "Used to be" is, after all, a common idiom for "ought to be."

Gould shows how Indian groups, as they rose against the British raj a century ago, tried to restore the rule of native kings and princes, no matter how feeble or reluctant these men were. To an outsider, the Indians' goals looked impossible. Their transcending-transforming image was a composite and glorified vision of the pre-British past. Even if it could have been institutionalized—in spite of Anglo capacity for overkill—it would not bring back a world empty of England. It might, however, produce a "used to be" parity of power and, just as important, a parity of cultural legitimacy between Anglo and Indian. Indians probably were uncertain as to the forms this parity would take but certain that such forms would emerge.

Here we encounter an overlap between utopian activism on the one hand and forms such as nativism or acculturation on the other. Often the utopian, too, claims no clear picture of the transcendent world and offers only a few guidelines for its construction. In self-effacement, he may even claim that, because history has tainted him as much as other men, he cannot presume to know more than a few such principles, and so should not prescribe programs or draw blueprints. Let people just begin to apply his principles, and utopia will begin to emerge. In conference discussions, Robert Boguslaw termed this a heuristic or psychedelic style of planning, a sort of faith in cultural "happenings."[5]

One difference is apparent. The utopian is aware of, and *deliberate* about, his intentions to produce a system that will be utterly new (witness the term "intentional community"). The nativist may not be. So perhaps we could distinguish utopians from other activists in terms of conscious intent to be creative. This would rephrase our problem somewhat, as one dealing with the social sources of consciousness and intent. I had this in mind, in part, in taking the title I have given this book.

This poses many problems. You can glimpse some of these by pairing Gould's essay with Love's section on the Alianza movement. Both the Alianzistas and the Indian "mutineers" saw fit to articulate their aims in traditional symbols. Love takes these symbols more or less at face value, as evidence of "primitive rebellion." Gould, on the other hand, sees creative potential behind them. Each point of view is productive; both authors teach us a great deal about the two movements. I hope, though, that in time they will also look at other contemporaneous movements in similar vein. What is there about the milieu of nineteenth-century India or twentieth-century New Mexico that discourages a *conscious* intent to build a different way of life? And if such a conscious intent were present, what difference might it make?

George L. Hicks takes up another facet of the awareness prob-

[5] See also Robert Boguslaw, *The New Utopians: A Study of Systems Design and Social Change* (Englewood Cliffs, N.J.: Prentice-Hall, 1965).

lem. How, he asks, does a utopian activist preserve his self-image as a builder of the better world when he encounters sluggishness, setbacks, and even failure? Part of the answer lies in the very imprecise and psychedelic quality of much utopian image-work, as is true for Banner community. Failures are more difficult to recognize. But another crucial part of the answer—as Hicks shows with much detail—is found in the existence of networks of fans and sympathizers. Though distant from Banner, they offer a pool of motivational insurance to its members. Ignoring the fact that Banner hasn't yet gotten anywhere, network people encourage community members to go on thinking of themselves as creative dissenters in a hostile world.

The networks also supply recruits to Banner and send information about utopian activism elsewhere. Hicks mentions a considerable number of wandering utopians, drifting from one group to another which they hope will be better. Maren Lockwood finds this to be true of nineteenth-century American utopianism; I have noticed it also in present-day Japan. Someone should try—though it would be a mammoth task—to investigate such utopian "streams" en bloc, treating particular groups and communes as mere surface manifestations. A study of this sort could prepare the way for further inquiry into problems of utopian awareness. That is, many utopians also become involved in other forms of activism—Bannerites join urban peace marches, Kagawa in Japan organized a whole spectrum of different movements. Is this true as well of "primitive rebels"? Love seems to suggest that it is true at least of Tijerina and the Alianza leaders, though not of the rank-and-file. How does this kind of movement-sampling affect the chances that a *utopian* group will be institutionalized, rather than some other kind? Or that a group may shift from an unconscious to a conscious determination to create a radically new order, to "go utopian"?

These essays are but a beginning. Every reader will think of other points of view, other problems to pursue with regard to the awareness of utopias. We hope that this collection, like the utopian's pilot-plant commune, will have a good demonstration effect. For utopia may be an outlandish place, but awareness of it brings on urgent domestic problems.

4. *Economic Development as a Modern Utopia*

J O S E P H   G U S F I E L D
University of California, San Diego

Whether we view it narrowly or broadly, the concept of utopia points to how the imagination of the future affects the present. The push and the direction given by the mirage ahead prods us to continue on the road. In this paper, utopianism has a broader meaning than that of utopian communities, such as Owenites or kibbutzim. We are interested here in those visions of the future which appear as components of large-scale social movements, especially those that now involve total nations moving through history toward some fixed vision of a future.

Yet we do not wish to substitute the vague sense of a future good for the limited version of utopia as local and specific, a place in space and time. The criticism that "utopia" is a shapeless and empty word unless confined to literary products and particular planned communities has merit. There is a midpoint, however, which considers present events and patterns as aimed toward an ideal future, although not as detailed as the here and now of separate communal establishments. In talking about economic development in the new nations of Asia, Africa, and Latin America, we will suggest that the image of modernity provides just such a utopian description of the future—a description which has the transforming effect which we see as the consequence of utopian ideas in many forms.

As Karl Mannheim wrote, one of the characteristics of utopian thought is its situationally transcendent character which enables it to have a transforming effect on the existing historical order.[1] This transforming effect indicates how it is that the model of the future society acts to direct present action and at the same time transforms the orientations, the attitudes, and the aspirations of those who participate in utopian movements. The transcendent quality also contains the idea of going beyond what is present into some future state; e.g. in a "leap from the kingdom of necessity to the kingdom of freedom." Utopias do not seem logical and immediate steps from what is in existence at present. It is this latter sense in which Engels saw utopianism as a contrast to the historical necessities which Marxist thought utilized as a source of predictions.[2] The utopian vision, in this sense, breaks with historical continuity. A utopia is therefore mythic and, insofar as it is, it can unlock energies that make possible what seemed only a short time before so difficult to attain.

In addition to its *transforming* and *transcendental* character, there are two other aspects of utopian thought that also emerge as elements directing large-scale political or social action. One of

[1] Karl Mannheim, *Ideology and Utopia*, trans. Louis Wirth and Edward Shils (New York: Harcourt, Brace and Co., 1949), pp. 173–84.
[2] Frederich Engels, *Socialism: Utopian and Scientific* (New York: International Publishers, Inc., 1968).

these is the *eschatological* notion of an end, sometimes more clearly conceived than at other times, but at all times with some sense of a goal toward which movement is possible. This means that the utopian element here is ideological in Mannheim's larger sense of the mobilization of thought into systems and consequent programs; it is a detailed statement of what is to be achieved. The planner's statements of his imagined ideal city are programs for achievement, utopias meant to stir and direct activity. In this sense, we can contrast a vague notion of the future with a specific and particular one; we can talk of political movements that have their "City of God" and those that lack it.

The final aspect of utopian thought in large-scale political movements is its *totalistic* character. Most writers on social change have tried to make some typology of social movements that distinguish between small-scale and large-scale movements, between those that deal with a specific rule or law and those that are far-reaching and involve institutional systems and/or major values. The distinction here is between a movement for women's suffrage and the general feminist movement to emancipate women in many areas. The former sought a specific kind of reform; the latter sought a total change in the conception or definition of women in this society. Political utopias, in being totalistic, are parts of revolutionary thinking.

As construed above, the problem of utopianism at times seems to be a uniquely Western one. We have described utopian ideals in ways which emphasize their *transforming* effect on present action, their *transcendental* quality of going beyond what is possible today, their *eschatological* view of goals, and their revolutionary significance in suggesting *total* change. Scholars reflecting on the experiences of non-Western civilization have sometimes considered that utopian ideas have little political significance in the societies of non-European history. Some of the papers in this volume touch on this issue.[3] In recent years, the study of millenarian and messianic movements in Oceania and in Africa has suggested that such movements may become affected with political significance in the form of nationalistic and independence ventures. As we consider the impact of a surge toward economic development in the post–World War II world, we will suggest that this view of a wide hiatus between East and West has less and less validity today.

Let me backtrack a little, however, from this general statement about utopianism to consider the related issue of politicization. In his famous essay on world religions, Max Weber distinguishes several ways in which religions respond to common problems of the tension between spiritual and worldly values.[4] His famous distinction between innerworldly and otherworldly asceticism is one way of saying that religions transcend the social order in different ways; given the sense of rejection of the social order, one way to transcend it is to detach oneself from it and lead an ascetic life apart from routine and prosaic existing. The monk or the holy man exemplifies this. Another pattern lies in attempting to overcome or remake this world into one closer to the ideal image. Weber's essay presents a set of logical possibilities by which a social order can be rejected or by which it can be transcended to a new one. Heaven, too, can be seen as a utopia.

Robert Merton, in his classic essay on "Social Structure and Anomie," discussed a similar problem.[5] He considered a number of different activities which have interested students of social

[3] See especially the discussion of this issue in the paper by Seiji Nuita (Ch. 1).

[4] Max Weber, "Religious Rejections of the World and Their Direction," in H. H. Gerth and C. Wright Mills, eds., *From Max Weber* (New York: Oxford University Press, 1946), esp. pp. 323–27.

[5] Robert Merton, *Social Theory and Social Structure* (Glencoe, Ill.: Free Press, 1949), pp. 125–50.

problems, such as crime, alcoholism, vice, drug use, rebellion, and other forms of what we used to call "social disorganization." He tried to find a paradigm for these through the discrepency between means and ends in American society, suggesting that in America all social classes share a common set of culture values. People strive for success in monetary and in status terms, but some people have better chances at this than others. For some, an opportunity structure exists which makes it easy to attain the goals which others, blocked by a less open opportunity structure, find less attainable. The poor commit more crimes than the rich because other ways of gaining money and status are closed to them. Thus crime is a rejection of legitimate means, because such means are not available to the criminal. Other people, for a variety of sociological reasons, take other routes. The alcoholic retreats from the race by his illness. Some give up the effort to achieve the ends but continue to perform all the actions of striving with few expectations of rewards. The "ritualists" do not expect to gain the ends of their society, but they plug along anyway. They are what Everett Hughes calls the "thank God for people" who work hard and don't ask for a raise.

Surprisingly, Merton says very little in his essay about rebellions or about utopias. It is implicit in his paradigm, and he recognizes it as a logical possibility; from our vantage point, it is another way of looking at the possibilities inherent in the combinations of rejection of the legitimacy of a social order.

When, then, do people band together to seek change politically, and what is the role which a political utopia plays for them at that time? Certainly Merton's retreatist or Weber's inner-worldly ascetic have appeared many times in the past. The use of drugs or religious exaltation to reach points of ecstasy, the heightening of sexual promiscuity in the form of group behavior, the religious and mystical movements, have many analogs in history to the contemporary hippie communes,[6] Sexual Freedom League, or Timothy Leary's admonition to "tune in, turn on, drop out." Movements of withdrawal are in many ways manifestations of that inner detachment so classically imputed to Eastern philosophy; the world is inherently evil, and man adapts to it by detaching himself from worldly desires and human sensitivities. His activities in the world no longer become crucial to him. "Look to the lilies of the field. They toil not; neither do they spin."

So, too, men may individually react to this disaffection and disappointment by self-abnegation. Studies of college dropouts in American society have frequently shown that they blame their failures on themselves, rather than on the institution—its standards, its grading practices, and the kinds of skill which are demanded. Today, in the United States, we are witnessing a shift in this as students and others come to politicize the educational structure and turn individual fate into political action. At this point, the utopian vision becomes significant.

It is obvious, too, that the withdrawal movement may, in turn, take a form which is itself utopian in the narrower sense; that is, to separate from the society and form a new community. Historically, this has happened by groups "handling" their discontent with inegalitarian structures by developing new religious sects, such as the Sikhs did in India, or as characterized by the Bhakti movement in India, and as is typical in the development of Methodism or Baptism in England or the United States.

The efforts of Jews to find their new Jerusalem in the old, of blacks to seek their own society, or of the French Canadians to proclaim independence all provide instances of varying forms of nationalistic utopias. Theodor Herzl, more than anyone else "the father of Zionism," put it in his picture of the Zionist fu-

[6] See the various movements described in Norman Cohn, *The Pursuit of the Millennium* (New York: Harper Torchbooks, 1961), esp. Chs. 6–9.

ture, *Der Judenstadt,* when he said that the Jews would have their own Champs Élysée and Arc de Triomphe.

It is in this latter sense (analogous to nationalist movements of minorities in the West) that the idea of modernity infuses a utopian spirit into the history of new nations and underdeveloped areas in the present world. The sense of the nation moving toward a highly specific goal is unique to the contemporary period in world history. It is not only that the elite of new nations have a concept of modernity as a goal toward which one strives, but that modernity exists as a present possibility: a technological character of the industrialized society. You can walk down an Indian street in a provincial city and find an ox-cart, a bicycle, automobiles, an airplane going overhead, an air-conditioned building going up, and wonder what American politics would have been like in the 1850's if we had had a clear conception of the 1960's.

This is what is possible in developing areas today. There is a very clear conception of a possible future which gives direction and issue to current actions. The present, as it exists in the world, is also a future for others in the same world. It is this that gives a utopian character to politics in new nations today. It is often around this character of the future as a possibility that a great many movements occur.

The discussion of development and modernization is essentially a post–World War II phenomenon. It is a function of the developed independence of new nations, as well as the interest and sentiment with which the advanced industrial societies have approached them. Looking back on the history of western nations, we sometimes impute forms of rational decision-making about the future which are often belied by the concrete, muddled events in which people acted. The situation is, indeed, much closer to this when we look at the self-conscious efforts to transform societies. The best instance of this occurred in the nineteenth century, in the Japanese Meiji restoration of 1868. Here, an entire nation was specifically seeking transformation in the direction of a thoroughly explicit kind of vision—to modernize, with Western society as a technological model. In spite of all the qualifications that one would have to make for this inspiring of the peculiar blend of tradition and modernity in the history of Japan, nevertheless, there was a point in time and a set of characteristics when the Japanese elite tried to move their society along in a particular direction and toward a specific technological utopia.

The same phenomenon—of the nation considered as a social movement and modernity as a utopia—has been seen in the countries that have achieved independence since 1945. The national plan, the community development program, and the agency for reconstruction all are efforts to transform the society. The goal of modernity may involve shifts of political or religious institutions, but it tends to be one or another version of what is to be found in Western societies—whether the model be Eastern or Western Europe. One cannot be in Bombay without recognizing London in embryo.

The symbols of modernity become necessary as trappings of the inner aspirations. Every country wants to have its own hardware, its own steel industry, its own airlines. While these have explanations in terms of national interests and economic efficiency, they also are seen as proof of the direction of the society. The modern utopia emerges out of the awareness which the modernizers have of this existent state and goal.

There are two ways in which this utopianism meets resistance. One is in the form of counter-utopianism. I am more familiar with these in India than elsewhere, but such are by no means traditional. Gandhi was quite explicit in his attempts to shuck off the modernistic and the Western and to build up the village along lines of harmony, personal relationships, and emotional security—all things he felt disappearing in the West.

By and large, political and bureaucratic planners in underdeveloped areas have not bought the Gandhian effort. Communitarian movements, such as the Sarvodaya movement of Vinoba Bhave and Jayaprakash Narayan, have had only a modest impact in India. Such movements have been specifically non-political, seeking to transform people through a direct appeal. Vinoba, for example, attempted to get landlords to give up land for the village and poor tenants.

Communitarianism has represented a turning away from the efforts to transform the total nation by political and economic plan; it is a move back into the local and limited conception of utopian development. Here the communitarian ideal emerges as a critique of the political effort to transform institutions. The communitarian maintains that one cannot bring about transformation in a society without transforming the kinds of persons in it. This utopia is anti-bureaucratic and, at best, anti-urban and anti-modern.

There is a second limitation to the utopianism implicit in modernization. It stems, not from a counter-utopia, but from the political activity which in itself is unleashed by a nationalistic effort. The development of industrial societies and political nations in the West was accompanied by considerable expansion of political participation by a variety of social and economic classes in a society. As various groups begin to participate in a total society, they substitute organized movements of political reform for apathy or explosive social protest. The development of independence movements and the rise of new nations have been coupled with a similar kind of change. In the Indian context, the one which I know best, this has had an explosion into the political arena. Various social groups in the forms of caste, region, religious community, and linguistic segments have utilized the new forms of political democracy to create areas for their competitive strivings.[7] As this has happened, politics has become more populistic, reaching down into what someone has called the "rice roots" of the society, making appeals increasingly on the basis of hard political interests and involving the bargains and trades of the various social segments with each other.

Such movements draw politics away from the tense drama of the independence movements and the force of the intellectual elites who forged their ideas in contact with Western industrial society. These trends to interest-group politics lessen the extent to which the utopia of modernity is actively at work in underdeveloped areas in their post-independence periods. The view of the nation as a consistent whole, moving in a similar direction, and the utopian image of the present Western industrial society as the future of the new nation, is less and less capable of transforming groups within the society in the day-to-day battle of political gain and loss. The game of politics, political interests, and organization with the day-to-day stress of political interests replaces the utopian view of an attainable society different from the present. It becomes harder and harder for appeals to be made to people about the future of the society. The very fact that political institutions are becoming more participatory and open tends to increase the role that reformist and ameliorative movements will play and undercuts the capability of a utopian ideal to produce leadership and a united following.

I end on a problem rather than a conclusion: Is utopianism, in the sense of an explicit future which transforms people, compatible with the existence of institutions of wide political participation? Is the existence of institutions in which conflict is regulated, and in which immediate and day-to-day compromises

[7] See Myron Weiner, *The Politics of Scarcity* (New Delhi: Asia Publishing House, 1963).

ameliorate discontents, compatible with the total spirit of a national utopianism?

Perhaps the nineteenth-century American communitarians and the contemporary followers of Gandhi or Buber must be taken most seriously in their belief that the transforming capacity of utopias is best conducted outside of political institutions. Alongside the state, as Gandhi believed, it was necessary to have men who sought to change others by the force of their vision and the exemplary life with which they brought that vision into existence on a small scale. Such men do not seek to change laws, or create new institutions, but to transform society by transforming attitudes and feelings in an essentially apolitical fashion: by a utopian appeal.

5. *The Utopian Side of the Indian Uprising*

HAROLD GOULD
University of Illinois, Urbana

I

The uprising against the British East India Company rule in 1857 was one of the most violent episodes in Indian history, yet it has

I am grateful to the various agencies and institutions which have supported my India work over the years and have thereby made possible what has been done here. These include: the Institute of International Education for a Fulbright Scholarship in 1954–55, the National Science Foundation for a Post-Doctoral Fellowship in 1959–60, the National Institute of Mental Health for Post-Doctoral Fellowships in 1960–61 and 1961–62, the University of Pittsburgh for an Andrew Mellon Post-Doctoral Fellowship in 1962–63, the American Institute of Indian Studies for a Faculty Research Fellowship in 1966–67, and the Midwest Universities Consortium for International Activities for a Research Fellowship for the summer of 1969. All of these grants and fellowships, except the Mellon Fellowship, permitted me to do research in India.

proved to be one of the most difficult for historians to interpret. Typical of the analytical difficulties involved is Michael Edwardes's recent attempt to summarize the causes and factors which contributed to the making of this complex event. Says he:

> Essentially, the mutiny which had been triggered by disaffections in the Bengal army was a feudal reaction to the pressures of British dominion which had been felt at all levels of the community. Behind the rebels were temporarily coalesced a wide and conflicting range of interests. There has been much controversy— engendered in the main by Indian historians—about the "national" character of the Mutiny. There was none. Among the feudal elements involved, there was merely a desire to return to things as they had been before the coming of the British. The sepoys rebelled in what they believed was self-defense. Not unnaturally, other elements took advantage of the breakdown of law and order. In some areas, there were distinctly Luddite overtones when mobs attacked and destroyed factories and machinery. This may well have been partly a product of class antagonisms.[1]

Technically, then, the 1857 uprising was a mutiny among sepoys of the Bengal army, which began at Meeruth, near Delhi, on May 10. It spread rapidly to most of the Gangetic plain, from the edge of the Punjab to the border of Bengal, and southward to the edge of the Deccan plateau. Culturally speaking, however, as Edwardes suggests, the uprising was something more than a mere mutiny in the armed forces, because it also implicated a variety of categories in the Indian population in ways and to an extent implying the prevalence of widespread social discontent throughout the country. Yet, as Edwardes rightly concludes, there is virtually no solid evidence to suggest any validity to the contemporary nationalist assertion that this uprising was the kind of

---

[1] Michael Edwardes, *Raj* (London: Pan Books, 1967), p. 78.

articulate demand for justice, reform, and freedom that would qualify it as an authentic "freedom movement."

If the uprising was more than a mutiny and less than a freedom movement, then what, precisely, was it? I believe it is possible to discern an underlying order and purpose in this uprising if one is prepared to go beyond conventional history and adopt a perspective which anthropologists have pioneered. This perspective has arisen from the observation of cultures under extreme duress. In modern times, the chief cause of this phenomenon has been the technological and demographic expansion of the West into the remainder of the world. By achieving such dramatic success for more than three centuries in imposing their economic and political systems upon people of every kind and level, the countries of the West posed a problem of cultural survival to many of the societies which fell under their domination. The desperate response of the members of these societies to what rightly appeared to be the threat of cultural extinction frequently took the form of social upheavals which anthropologists call "revitalization movements." Such movements were strongly utopianistic in that they promised the removal of their society's European tormentors by one miraculous means or another and a renewal of the native way of life in its most idealistically conceivable terms. As chaotic, sporadic, and irrational as these movements may have seemed to colonial soldiers, administrators, and conventional historians alike, their anthropological investigation invariably reveals a remarkable consistency in form, purposes, and conditions of manifestation. Speaking of revitalization movements in a classic formulation of the subject, Anthony F. C. Wallace called them deliberate, organized, conscious efforts by the members of a society to construct a more satisfying culture. He continues:

> Revitalization is thus, from a cultural standpoint, a special kind of culture change phenomenon: the persons involved . . . must

perceive their culture, or some major areas of it, as a system (whether accurately or not); they must feel that this cultural system is unsatisfactory; and they must innovate not merely discrete items, but a new cultural system, specifying new relationships as well as, in some cases, new traits.[2]

Due to their primary interest in so-called simpler or tribal societies, the empirical cases out of which anthropologists like Wallace built their concept of the revitalization movement inevitably led to their stressing those features of such movements that were common at this cultural level. James Mooney was probably the discoverer of the revitalization movement, in the sense of being the first to attempt a systematic explanation of the phenomenon, and his was a lucid description of the Ghost Dance among disintegrating American Plains Indian cultures toward the end of the nineteenth century.[3] Studies of the cargo cults that arose among the aboriginal tribes of Melanesia under the impact of Western imperialism followed after the 1920's, and soon a descriptive and analytical literature on bizarre social upheavals among primitive cultures had acquired a respectable scientific status in the anthropological establishment.[4] Ralph Linton's essay on nativistic movements[5] and Wallace's on revitalization movements were early attempts at conceptual synthesis in this area, but attempts that were necessarily limited by their reference almost exclusively to data from aboriginal sources. This is a point to which I will revert after I have gone more deeply into the case of the Indian upris-

---

[2] Anthony F. C. Wallace, "Revitalization Movements," *American Anthropologist* 58 (1966):265.

[3] James Mooney, *The Ghost Dance Religion among the Indians of the Western Plains* (Berkeley and Los Angeles: University of California Press, 1951).

[4] See Peter M. Worsley, *The Trumpet Shall Sound* (New York: Schocken Books, 1968); also Peter Lawrence, *Road Belong Cargo* (Manchester: Manchester University Press, 1964).

[5] Ralph Linton, "Nativistic Movements," *American Anthropologist* 45 (1943):230–40.

ing. For now, it will be sufficient to reiterate that the Indian uprising of 1857 looks less like a hodgepodge of haphazard, unrelated events and more like an underlyingly ordered social phenomenon, when it is subjected to the analytical conventions employed by students of revitalization movements.

I I

As a prelude to our consideration of the 1857 uprising, we may profitably contemplate a passage from Mooney's inquiry into the Ghost Dance religion. It poignantly captures the atmosphere of mingled distress, anxiety, and utopianistic fantasy in which revitalization movements everywhere have arisen. Says he:

> . . . the lost paradise is the world's dreamland of youth. What tribe or people has not had its golden age. . . . And when the race lies crushed and groaning beneath an alien yoke, how natural is the dream of a redeemer, an Arthur, who shall return from exile or awake from some long sleep to drive out the usurper and win back for his people what they have lost. The hope becomes a faith and the faith becomes the creed of priests and prophets, until the hero is a god and the dream a religion, looking to some great miracle of nature for its culmination and accomplishment. . . .[6]

Against this background, let us now analyze the rebellion of the Indian sepoys against their employers, the British East India Company. As we shall see, their rebellion was the by-product and the understandable focal point of a kind of millenarian dream which had slowly taken hold of vast multitudes of Indians, particularly in the more isolated inland reaches of the subcontinent, and which finally impelled them to hurl themselves against their

[6] Mooney, *Ghost Dance Religion*, p. 1.

alien masters with a fury that for a brief time compensated for their lack of either modern weapons or leadership. The pathway to this violent and complex interlude in Indian history was paved by an incredible sequence of events by which an essentially commercial enterprise, a trading company owned by stockholders and governed by a board of directors, acting under a charter from the crown, achieved the status of an Indian dynasty. This process formally began exactly a century prior to the uprising, with the Battle of Plassey on June 23, 1757. Here Robert Clive, profiting from a most elaborate pattern of intrigues, overcame the forces of Siraj-ud-Daula, the Nawab (or king) of Bengal, with almost ridiculous ease.[7]

This victory, accomplished with a mixture of native and European troops, made it possible for the East India Company to obtain de facto control of Bengal's political establishment and make certain that Siraj's successor was willing to be subservient to British interests. Seven years later, in 1764, after enjoying less success than anticipated in stage-managing the conduct of the princes whom it had elected to support, and after having driven even their puppet nawab (Mir Kasim) into open hostility, the Company won a battle at Buxar which allowed it to assume direct suzerainty over this great and important eastern province of the decaying Moghul empire. Their new administration was rendered de jure after the Company sought and received from the titular head of the old Moghul empire in Delhi, Emperor Shah Alam II, the *diwani* (or right to collect the land revenue) of Bengal, Bihar, and Orissa (then forming the one great province of Bengal). With this legitimation in hand, the East India Company commenced the systematic exploitation of this region for

---

[7] The concrete historical events discussed in the paper can be explored in more detail in any of the standard histories of India. One good source is R. C. Majumdar, *An Advanced History of India* (London: McMillan, 1953).

its corporate benefit, as well as for the benefit of the traders and administrators in its employ. It also commenced a pattern of military and economic adventurism which carried the East India Company's dominance steadily up the Gangetic plain and southward into the Deccan plateau (while her Madras and Bombay enclaves were expanding according to their own regional opportunities), until the entire subcontinent had fallen effectively under its control.

As the East India Company's domain grew and its military and political power increased commensurately, the character of the confrontation between the British and native institutions began to undergo a major transformation. At first, the Company had been one among a plethora of regional dynasties in India which, in the wake of the Moghul collapse, had been engaged in minor wars and extensive intrigues in an effort to maximize their fortunes in relation to the others. Although life for the ordinary man was harsh and frequently lethal under these circumstances, the social and cultural life of most people continued to be conducted within the compass of political, religious, and economic institutions which had been traditional in India for as long as anyone could remember. But after the Mysore kingdom, the Mahratta confederacy, the Sikh monarchy, and the Hyderabad state, along with many lesser kingdoms, were subdued by East India Company arms and absorbed wholly or in part into her administrative domain, and when the Great Moghul at Delhi and the Nawab of Oudh became primarily English puppets, the confrontation between the British and the native populations of India ceased being a mere political episode and assumed the proportions of a cultural onslaught. This soon came to be perceived by the latter as threatening the extinction of Indian civilization itself: its religion, its domestic life, its political system, its status structure, its very sense of identity. Their response to this situation began to assume millenarian and utopianistic overtones.

The source of the anxiety and unrest which followed Company paramountcy lay in the procedures which the British authorities followed in their efforts to lay solid technological, economic, political, and juridical foundations for the vast domains they had acquired. The Bengal army became a center of the resultant ferment for a number of very good reasons. This was a mercenary force raised by the East India Company to enforce the authority of the Bengal presidency. Around the time of the mutiny, this army numbered 151,000, of which only 23,000 were Europeans; and only 10,000 of these were actually stationed on the Gangetic plain south of the Punjab. Most native recruits were taken from the high martial castes, the Brahman castes, and the Muslim communities resident in Agra, Oudh, and the Punjab. When millenarian discontent passed over into active hostilities, the sepoys alone had meaningful access to the weaponry and knowledge of military tactics and organization with which the Company's ascendancy had been made possible. It was also the sepoy whose confrontation with the mounting contradictions in the Indian's life, which the attempted tranformation of that ascendancy into a permanent state of affairs generated, was in many ways the most direct and immediately challenging. To put it another way, in the cultural confrontation between the British and the Indians, the sepoy regiments became more than merely military units; they became the major organizational confluence of an elaborate series of social networks which extended throughout the northern plains and into almost every native community. This *cultural* role played by the sepoy, utilizing the channels of communication and interaction facilitated by the Bengal army itself, and by the entire administrative and technological infrastructure (that is, the railways, the roads, the postal and telegraphic services) established by the Company, was one of the key elements of the 1857 uprising. In a very real sense, the sepoy became the chief articulator and instrument of a revitalization movement whose goal was to restore Indian life to a highly fantasized, utopianized conception of the glories it had known before the arrival of the hated *firingi*, the European. That it resembled other such movements in this and other respects is clear to anyone familiar with the relevant literature; that it revealed some important differences from the earlier "classical" formulations is also evident, and this fact will presently become the basis for whatever further contributions to theory this essay strives to make.

III

The immediate question, then, is: what were the circumstances surrounding the transformation of the sepoy recruits from a strictly military into a volatile cultural force? Despite differences among historians on the real nature of the 1857 uprising, there is remarkable agreement about the general conditions and policies which led to the final explosion.

Especially since the issuance of the *firman*, after 1764, which made the Company *diwan* of Bengal, the process of altering and displacing native cultural institutions in the interests of Company administration, finance, and commerce had proceeded, in native eyes at least, at an alarmingly rapid pace. Several classes in the populations of the old Moghul empire's heartland were feeling the pinch from changes in whose formulation they did not participate and of whose purposes they were profoundly suspicious. Most important of all, while the British tended to view the changes they were initiating mainly in legalistic and technical bureaucratic terms, the Indians whose interests and sense of security were being challenged by them tended to view them increasingly in cultural and ultimately in religious terms. No matter how reprehensible and repugnant such features of Indian cultural life as widow-burning (*sati*) or caste may have seemed to nineteenth-century Englishmen, they formed aspects of a coherent and ancient cultural tradition in India and were intimately tied to the deepest religious sensibilities. The fact that some of the reforms which the Company's government instituted from its capital in Calcutta were urged by the modernizing segment of the Bengali intelligentsia itself, which had experienced the longest and most intensive interaction with British customs, did not help the vast majority of the population outside Bengal to accept them. For there was already a continuum of acculturation reaching up the Ganges that was in inverse ratio to the distance from Company headquarters. The farther inland you went, the less deeply changes had penetrated; for this very reason, the impact of changes which did come were the more profoundly felt and responded to. And, most significantly in this regard, the soldiers of the Bengal army were recruited mainly from the less acculturated upper Gangetic region and not from the more acculturated Bengal region. As Chaudhuri has put it: ". . . in 1857 there was the greatest dislike of British authority where it had not yet been long established; and conversely, there was the least effort toward change in those parts of India which had longest been subject to British rule."[8]

One case of deep discontent, aside from the sepoys, whose specific complaints will be explored presently, were the political victims of the Company's ascendancy in the aftermath of the regional dynastic wars of the late eighteenth and early nineteenth centuries. Once all the loci of effective military and political opposition to Company rule had been subdued by firepower and intrigue, a policy of close control over the defeated regional elites and the princely families who exercised moral authority

[8] S. B. Chaudhuri, "The Union of the Civil and Military Rebellions," in Ainslee T. Embree, ed., *1857 in India* (Boston: D. C. Heath, 1963) p. 66.

over them was pursued. The regional elites were brought to heel by rationalizing the land tenure systems and making retention of economic privileges and their social concomitants dependent upon political quietude and faithful remittance of land revenues. An attempt was made to control the princes by settling them outside their traditional domains when they were thought to be too dangerous to be left within them, and by the so-called "doctrine of lapse." The latter came to mean, in effect, that any kingdom which the Company deemed to be no longer worthy of an independent existence, either because its administration had grown irreversibly incompetent or because its ruling family had not produced an heir which the Company recognized as legal, would be dissolved and absorbed into British-owned territory. To their victims, these procedures could hardly seem other than unjust, particularly in a cultural world where moral and political authority rested upon hereditary principles of legitimation rather than upon the performance qualities and impersonal legal principles espoused by the East India Company's representatives. Ironically, British good intentions and attitudes of fair play toward one's adversary had helped exacerbate this situation. The British had not, as others might have, totally shattered the power and prestige of the defeated princes; rather, they had simply tried to bar them from further exercising active political power while permitting them to retain significant quanta of personal property and wealth, often formidable entourages of kinsmen, courtiers, and body guards, and very generous incomes from their Company-managed treasuries. With such resources at their command, it proved possible for many disaffected princes, including those at the court of the Great Moghul in Delhi, to extend their networks of anti-British intrigue into the Bengal army, into the ranks of the restive and disenfranchised local elites, and into the councils of the Wahabi movement, an ultra-fundamentalist Muslim religious movement whose zealots sought a restoration of the old Islamic way of life.

Four events, more than any others, convinced the Indian princely class that the ultimate British intention was to eliminate them. These were the fates of the ruling houses of Poona, Jhansi, Oudh, and Delhi respectively. The Moghul throne in Delhi had survived for 150 years beyond the death of Aurangzeb, the last really viable emperor, more or less as the papacy has endured since the fall of the Roman empire. It remained the penultimate symbol of traditional cultural and political authority in India, to which all manner of local and regional power-holders turned for legitimation. We saw how Clive did so when he wanted to put an official stamp on the Company's conquest of Bengal. But when the heir-apparent to Bahadur Shah II (the blind and aesthetic contemporary occupant of the throne) died, the British authorities decreed that the Moghul crown would lapse after the demise of its present wearer. This news filled the royal court with dismay and discontent, because it thwarted the hopes for succession of several collateral kinsmen and their entourages who had anticipated that the surcease of Bahadur Shah's line meant renewed opportunities for their own.

After his defeat by the British in 1817, Peshwa Baji Rao II, the leader of the Mahratta confederacy, was removed from his capital at Poona and allowed to settle on the banks of the Ganges near Kanpur, a thousand miles to the north. Upon his death in 1851, an adopted son called Nana Sahib succeeded him; but the Company refused to permit him to use the dynasty's official seal and made it clear they were no longer prepared to acknowledge the house's continuation beyond the lifetime of its present head. In 1854, the kingdom of Jhansi was incorporated into the British domains, after the Company refused to allow succession by adoption. The Rani of Jhansi, regent for the adopted minor, was compelled to accept this edict and was pensioned off despite powerful protests and protracted litigation which carried all the way to London. And finally, Wajid Ali Shah, the Nawab of Oudh, in some ways the last independent remnant of the old Moghul heartland, was deposed and deported to Calcutta and his kingdom dissolved in 1856 on the grounds that its administration had totally broken down and its rulers had grown completely dissolute. This last act by Governor-General Dalhousie, who had determined to use the "doctrine of lapse" as an instrument for deliberately enlarging the scope of the Company's Indian empire, was probably the most decisive of all in convincing segments of the nobility that they must pursue desperate measures to save the cultural system which sustained their prerogatives and their hopes of eventual restitution. British policies had at once struck at the descent system (a fundamental cultural structure everywhere) and at the very idea of monarchy in its Indian manifestation as an ultimate legitimizer of status, and patron and regulator of religion. It was interpreted as a systematic effort to destroy the Indian elite by destroying its political and cultural foundations.

Simultaneously, British reforms aimed at the wider society, either out of sincere interest in its betterment or in the interest of modernizing the technology of administration and commerce, had a similar effect of generating a general sense of cultural peril. We have already suggested that the banning of widow immolation and some curbs upon the excesses of caste were even urged by the modernizing sector of the Bengali elite and primarily concurred in by the Company administration; yet they were no less regarded as attacks on Indian culture and religion by the majority who believed implicitly in those customs. The suppression of the *thuggees*[9] was misunderstood in some quarters,

[9] The *thuggees* were a specialized caste of thieves who preyed upon travelers. They worshipped Kali, and would strangle their victims with a silken cord after going to elaborate lengths to win their confidence.

despite its laudability from the vantage of liberal society. When Christian missionaries got permission to come out to India and propagate the faith under tacit Company protection, the sense of cultural onslaught grew still more acute. It was further heightened by the spread and intensification of evangelical styles of Christianity among the general English population and, by extension, among all levels of the Company's personnel. "After 1820," says Michael Edwardes, "the evangelical Christianity of many of the Company's officers led them to see evil in almost everything." He continues:

> The atmosphere in which the land itself was an enemy certainly affected the judgment of many. It reinforced their dislike of India, and explained too, the occasional outbursts of hysteria among the British population.
>
> By the 1850's, the British had virtually institutionalized their contempt for things Indian. Their sense of duty was fully supported by a militant Christianity. . . . By 1857, it was generally felt by British officials in India that Indians were a pretty evil lot and it was Britain's duty to civilize and Christianize them. . . .[10]

Unquestionably sensitive people among the Indian population became aware of this contempt and the cultural implications it was coming to have, especially when suspicions were being confirmed by visible events. Act 21 of 1850 separated property rights from ritual obligations and decreed that Christian converts could henceforth inherit ancestral property. The Hindu Widows Remarriage Act was formulated before the mutiny (although not activated until afterward) and obviously attacked the authority of orthodox Hinduism. The building of roads and railways meant the violation of tracts of land held sacred by various communities and, often, the destruction or relocation of religious structures. Rail travel, furthermore, could not be

---

[10] Edwardes, p. 51.

economically organized to accommodate the intricacies of caste differentiation, with the result that the inevitable caste-mixing which occurred on the railways got interpreted as a cunning conspiracy to dilute and destroy the caste system. The same interpretation was placed upon the practice of common messing in the jails and the suspension of *purdah* and other socially exclusive practices in the name of scientific medicine in hospitals.

What is perhaps most important about the process described here was its cumulative quality. Not one incident, policy, or accidental offense to native sensibilities was in itself sufficient to create an overwhelming sense of cultural crisis. But the overall impact of such a plethora of things, all of which appeared to the native society to be pointing in the same direction, did ultimately succeed in generating this sensation. British and Indian historians alike have speculated that a "conspiracy" of some kind lay behind the uprising, without stopping to realize that from the Indian side the pattern of events leading to the explosion appeared equally to be a conspiracy fomented by the British acting through the East India Company, the military, and the missionary organizations, against the very fabric of Indian culture. Thus if some Indians, perhaps some of the disaffected princes in particular, hatched a conspiracy of their own, it was at the least understandable. However, the evidence suggests that spontaneous utopianistic response to a collapsing cultural world was by far the most compelling dimension of the people's behavior.

IV

But it was the sepoy upon whom the storms of cultural contradiction broke most violently and decisively. The sepoys were Hindus, Muslims, and Sikhs who found themselves part of a military force that was in the employ of the British East India Company, that was led by professional British military personnel, and that was expected to conform to the letter of the British military code. The latter is important, because it meant that the sepoy was regarded as being entirely *British* as far as his soldierly obligations were concerned, regardless of what his cultural identity might be. This is why I say that the cultural contradictions that were ramifying generally into the Indian society of the 1850's were impinging with special force upon the sepoy. For him, trying to preserve his cultural integrity and religious conscience ultimately meant risking denunciation as a traitor by his British masters.

Signs of what was to come appeared as early as 1806 in the Madras presidency. When Governor-General Sir George Barlow permitted the Madras army to abolish the *tikka* (forehead decorations), circumscribe beards, and introduce turbans with a leather cockade, a serious mutiny broke out at Vellore. In 1824, there was a mutiny at Barrackpore in Bengal when the Company broke its promise to the sepoys that they would never be sent for military duty outside India, which in those days was tantamount to being outcasted. Incidents of this kind multiplied over the years but might never in themselves have led so decisively to the congealing of the sepoys into a revitalistic force had it not been for the British decision in 1857 to replace the old musket called Brown Bess with the new more efficient Enfield rifle. The bullet used in this rifle was coated with grease and wrapped in tissue. To remove this tissue so the bullet could be loaded into the rifle, the top of it had to be bitten off; and when rumors spread through the Army that the grease employed was a mixture of beef and swine fat, its effects upon the Hindu mercenaries (who revered the cow) and the Muslim mercenaries (who abhorred the pig) can be easily imagined. Despite assurances that the grease was compounded of vegetable products and beeswax, and despite threats (which were frequently carried out) of harsh penalties for breach of the military code (by refusing commands to use the cartridges), restiveness in the native regiments literally surged toward a fever pitch. The greased cartridges became the universal symbol of cultural aggression; it was a summatory statement of how near at hand the Indian soldier believed cultural disintegration to be. The response of the British military authorities to this dangerous restiveness was to confront it with an equal and opposite measure of cultural chauvinism. Sepoys whose religious convictions made it impossible for them to obey the order to bite the cartridge wrappers were summarily tried and humiliated in front of their fellow soldiers "as an example," regardless of how loyally and bravely they may have served the army until that point. Other units which had refused orders en masse were dissolved and sent home. The effects of these measures were to demonstrate to the sepoys the inevitability of being compelled to choose between cultural survival and physical survival, and to diffuse back into the villages of Agra and Oudh—whence most of the victims had come—hundreds of discharged mercenaries who could merge their despair with that of their kinsmen, their co-religionists, and the local traditional elite. Organized plots by some of the major princes, like Nana Sahib at Kanpur, the nephews of Bahadur Shah II at Delhi, the Rani at Jhansi, and the Begum of Wajid Ali Shah (who was not exiled with her husband) at Lucknow, and the fundamentalist political aspirations of the Wahabi organization, were undoubtedly beneficiaries of the atmosphere of impending cultural doom which had seized the population in the wake of the horror which the greased-cartridge incidents had reaped within the army. These could supply organizational rubrics for what was otherwise a vast quantity of amorphous, yet volatile, discontent. But it is one thing to see these as the *beneficiaries* of a condition which was essentially created by others, and it is quite another to see them as the instigators or the cause of the condition. The latter, of course, is what the votaries of both "conspiracy" and "war of national independence" maintain; I contend that the revitalistic nature of the uprising makes it far more probable that the former was actually the case. But more about this later.

V

It is patently clear that as the sense of cultural peril rose and diffused among the Indian populace, especially in the Gangetic belt which had formed the core of the Moghul empire, a critical point was reached where some sort of millenarian restiveness began to grip both the military cantonments and the general countryside. British officials themselves could not help but notice it, at least vaguely, as shown in a most amazing letter written by Septimus Harding Becher to Captain E. M. Martineau on April 13, 1857:

> . . . We make a mistake in supposing that because we dress, arm and drill Hindustani soldiers as Europeans, they become one bit European in their feelings and ideas. I see them on parade for say two hours daily, but what do I know of them for the other 22?
>
> What do they talk about in their lines, what do they plot? . . .
>
> I know at the present moment an unusual agitation is pervading the ranks of the entire army, but what it will exactly result in, I am afraid to say. I can detect the near approach of the storm. . . . Everywhere, far and near, the army under some maddening impulse, are looking out with strained expectation for something, some unseen invisible agency has caused one common electric thrill to run thru' all.
>
> I don't think they know themselves what they will do, or that they have any plan of action except of resistance to invasion of

their religion and their faith. . . . If a flare-up from any cause takes place at one station, it will spread and become universal.[11]

Becher lacks the concepts and terminology to understand that he is describing the prelude to a revitalization movement. Yet he has sensed the existence of all the essential ingredients. He gropes for phraseology adequate to his needs, and he resorts to such phrases as "unusual agitation," "the near approach of the storm," "strained expectation," "one common electric thrill," and "resistance to invasion of their religion and faith." Confirmation of his fears was then only two months away at Meeruth; but even as he wrote, other poignant evidence of millenarian restiveness was already at hand. This was the appearance of strange, yet fascinating, millenarian symbolism among the general population.

Undoubtedly the most dramatic symbol was the phenomenon of the circulating *chapatis* (unleavened bread cakes). From January, 1857, from no identifiable source, one or two *chapatis*, each containing a lotus seed (symbol of regeneration in Hinduism), began to be delivered to the headmen of villages in the Gangetic plain, with an admonition that each headman receiving these *chapatis* should have similar ones prepared in his village and delivered in turn to the headmen of four or five surrounding villages, and so on. In this manner, thousands of villages received the message that deliverance from the *firingis* and regeneration of the traditional culture was near at hand.

Another symbolic manifestation was negative in character. This was the rumor of the rotten *atta* (flour), which in logical structure paralleled among the civilian population the greased-cartridge rumor among the sepoys. Like flames racing through dry tinder, the story spread across northern India that the *firingis* had been able to get powdered pig and cattle bones introduced

[11] J. A. B. Palmer, *The Mutiny Outbreak at Meerut in 1857* (Cambridge: The University Press, 1966), pp. 32–33.

into the supplies of flour being sold in the markets as a means of deliberately destroying the caste of every Hindu and the religious cleanliness of every Muslim. Once their religious status had been thereby destroyed, the belief went, all Indians would be compelled by the missionaries to become Christians, and Indian civilization would be at an end.

As previously noted, the final explosion occurred at Meeruth on May 10, 1857; the trigger was supplied by a martinet officer, Colonel Carmichael Smyth, who tried to compel ninety skirmishers selected from different troops of the Third Native Cavalry to set an example for all the soldiers on the cantonment by loading their rifles at a special parade called for the purpose. When eighty-five refused, they were arrested, tried, sentenced to ten years rigorous imprisonment, chained, and led off to jail before the entire assembled brigade. At 5 P.M. on May 10, a cook-boy ran through the native lines announcing that the Artillery and Rifles had seized their regimental arms and the Third Cavalry was en route to the jail to release their imprisoned comrades. After several hours of confusion and mayhem, mostly caused by the unleashing of the civilian population following the dissolution of law and order, the Meeruth sepoys marched off toward Delhi to offer themselves to the Moghul Emperor Bahadur Shah II, shouting, "The Company's Raj is over!" Within a month thereafter, every European had been swept clear of the entire region between Bengal, the Punjab, and the Deccan plateau, except for a body of Europeans and "loyal" sepoys who remained besieged at the residence in Lucknow for 140 days.

Within this vast zone, a spontaneous attempt was made by the sepoys to transfer their military skills from the foreign masters who had created them to representatives of the native elite whom it was believed would then use them to restore to India her traditional political, religious, and cultural forms. Their conception of these forms was a composite of dimly perceived and half-understood notions of what the India of yesteryear actually had been; what they were articulating was an inchoate yearning which many segments of the population, from princes to peasants, had developed for a cultural world devoid of pervasive inconsistency. The sepoys had unleashed a revitalization movement of sweeping proportions which had struck a responsive chord throughout much of northern India. Instead of giving rise to an individual prophet, or sequence of prophets, as was characteristic of such movements in primitive societies, in India the sepoys became *collective prophets* who turned to traditional leaders, the princes, with the plea—indeed, the *demand*—that they resume their ancient political roles. It is the failure to realize this, I believe, which has prevented students of the 1857 uprising from grasping its true nature.

Let us now examine this point more closely. I am suggesting that, although the uprising occurred superficially as a series of local mutinies by Bengal army mercenaries, they nevertheless conformed to an overall sociological pattern. Each one contained a set of common structural elements, not because a master conspiracy of princes and *wahabis* existed, but because all the rebelling sepoys and the general population who responded to their deed shared a common sense of cultural crisis and a common utopianistic stereotype of the kind of society required to allay that crisis. In this they resembled the state of affairs that existed in the Western Middle Ages which Norman Cohn describes so vividly: "So it came about that multitudes of people acted out with fierce energy a shared fantasy which though delusional yet brought them such intense emotional relief that they could live only through it and were perfectly willing to die for it. . . ."[12]

In virtually every known instance of sepoy mutinies, the fol-

[12] Norman Cohn, *The Pursuit of the Millennium* (New York: Harper Torchbooks, 1961), p. 74.

lowing sequence of events occurred: (1) The cantonment was seized, and the European officers and their staffs and families were either killed or allowed to make their way to British-controlled territory. (2) A period of rampage followed, in which sepoys and local civilians looted shops and possessions of dispatched Europeans and attacked symbols of European culture in, as Edwardes put it, Luddite fashion. (3) The sepoys marched to the palace of the local raja and compelled him, under pain of death where he was not spontaneously willing, to become their leader and with them establish some kind of government pledged to the restoration and preservation of the traditional cultural system.

In Meeruth, Delhi, Lucknow, Kanpur, and Jhansi, rebels followed this pattern precisely, as they did in most of the lesser-known uprisings. After expiating their immediate passions on the local cantonment, the Meeruth rebels struck out for Delhi and joined forces with their counterparts there. Together they descended on the Red Fort and demanded that Bahadur Shah II resume his status as Moghul emperor. When the old man pleaded inability to do so by reason of blindness, advanced age, and sheer disinclination, the sepoys threatened to kill him and his entire court. At this, Bahadur Shah agreed and made a sincere effort to establish some kind of administrative apparatus capable of managing the affairs of Delhi. At midnight on May 11, 1857, a twenty-one-gun salvo announced that a descendant of Babar (the first Moghul emperor) had once more ascended the throne of Delhi. All Europeans and Christian converts had by then been killed or driven from the city. Lacking any real experience in the technicalities of administration, the king and his advisors retained a facsimile of the organizational structure which the British had maintained in judicial, military, and revenue affairs. Since, under the near-chaotic conditions which prevailed, there could be little that resembled bureaucratically rational administration, almost all disputes regarding procedures to be followed, the redress of alleged injustices, etc., found their way to the throne for final disposition. Bakht Khan, who commanded the troops who mutinied at Bareilly and made their way to Delhi, ably augmented the old monarch's authority through the exercise of his considerable leadership abilities and political shrewdness. He appears to have been mainly instrumental in working out a modus operandi for managing the disparate, highly volatile elements which had converged on Delhi to demand that the throne fulfill their revitalistic fantasies. To placate the religious sensibilities of the Hindus in their ranks, for example, Bakht Khan successfully urged a prohibition against the slaughtering of cows under pain of the death penalty during the Muslim festival of Eed. The king himself set the example for this by sacrificing a sheep. In all, Delhi was free of Company control from May 11 to September 21, and during that time Hindus and Muslims collaborated in a touchingly naïve endeavor to revive the social world in which native cultural institutions could flourish once again.

At Kanpur the same basic pattern repeated itself, but with Nana Sahib as the focal point of the sepoys' affirmation of a revitalized native society. In some ways, the case of Nana Sahib is more remarkable, and more indicative of the revitalistic nature of the 1857 uprising, than that of Bahadur Shah II. Although a Hindu, Nana Sahib was a Maharashtrian Brahman, quite ethnically divorced from the Hindustani soldiers and civilians who turned to him for leadership. Yet, in the millenarian atmosphere that prevailed, this did not matter; what was important was that Nana Sahib represented the traditional political and religious orders. There is much evidence to suggest that the Maratha king was most reluctant to risk his considerable economic security (Rs 800,000 per year) over what was probably destined to be an abortive revolt against the mighty British empire. But once drawn into the vertex of the storm, Nana seems to have tried to rise to the occasion much in the same fashion as Bahadur Shah. He also made efforts to revive native institutions and to lead the native army which formed around him first, in coalition with Begum Hazrat's forces, against the English beseiged in the Lucknow residency and, later, against the avenging armies that descended on Oudh to suppress this uprising.

Both in Lucknow and Kanpur, which are only forty-five miles apart, the reforms instituted by the two leaders were typically revitalistic in nature. Nana agreed to a restoration of pre-annexation criminal law for his Hindu subjects and to a corresponding restoration of Islamic law. Begum Hazrat set up her minor son, Birjis Qadr, as successor to her husband on July 7, established herself as regent, and declared that Qadr's advisors were henceforth subservient to the Moghul throne at Delhi. The rebels fought ferociously under Nana and the Begum, but they lost in the end because they lacked the leadership and material to sustain their war against the resources of Great Britain. Nana Sahib was unrepentant until the end. He died a refugee in the wastes of the Nepal-India frontier region.

The last of the rebels whom I will consider here is the Rani of Jhansi. Although she has been elevated to the stature of a Joan of Arc by nationalist mythology, the Rani is much better understood as a revitalistic figure rather close to Nana Sahib, both in the circumstances which impelled her participation in the uprising and in her ultimate fate. Like the Begum Hazrat at Lucknow, the Rani's political status was derived from the regency of a son whom her husband adopted on his deathbed in a succession maneuver which neither the British authorities nor other segments of the royal family accepted. For these reasons, Dalhousie had incorporated Jhansi into British territories in 1857 and promised the Rani a liberal pension. The Rani appealed her case all the way to London and lost, as Nana had, and then resigned herself to a disgruntled "retirement."

In June, a servant of a sepoy leader in the Twelfth Native Infantry stationed at Jhansi brought a letter to the Rani stating that the entire Bengal army had risen against the British and that anyone failing to rise with them was either an outcaste or an infidel. On June 6, the Twelfth Native Infantry mutinied, seized the treasury containing Rs 450,000, and caused the Europeans in the area to flee into the large fort which is the central military feature at Jhansi. All were later massacred as they came out of the fort to surrender. Throughout these events, the Rani seems to have stayed in the background, fearful of being punished by the sepoys if she seemed unsympathetic and fearful of being punished by the British if she showed sympathy for or rendered support to them. She seems to have adopted a policy of trying to humor both sides and hoping for an eventual pathway out of her dilemma. Through the commander of the eventually massacred British refugees in the fort, she tried to induce their surrender by writing the following message: "What can I do? Sepoys have surrounded me, and say I have concealed the gentlemen, and that I must get the fort evacuated, and assist them. To save myself I have sent guns and my followers. If you wish to save yourselves, abandon the fort. No one will hurt you."[13]

The sepoys who committed the massacre then struck out for Delhi, as had their Meeruth counterparts, after extorting a large sum of money from the Rani. The British authorities, however, adjudged the Rani culpable for the massacre and declared her outlaw. She had little choice from that point on but to throw in with the uprising, which she did with apparent zeal. Like Nana Sahib, the Rani gradually molded herself to fit the role of revitalistic leader, and in the end she showed considerable skill and tenacity as a military commander. Eventually she was killed near Gwalior in 1858 while observing the course of a battle. From the

[13] Surendra Nath Sen, *1857* (New Delhi: Government of India, Publications Division, 1957).

beginning it seems very likely that the Rani of Jhansi, although disgruntled and not unwilling to see the demise of British power in India, was more the captive of a revitalistic upheaval than the promulgator of a dark conspiracy. Like her counterparts elsewhere, she was an embodiment of the traditional social order which the sepoys and the people were clamoring to have restored in order to relieve the sense of intolerable cultural inconsistency which beset them. Like Bahadur Shah, Nana Sahib, Begum Hazrat, and so many other members of the Indian princely class (whom space has not allowed us to discuss), the Rani was compelled by the force of the revitalistic fervor raging around her to merge her personality with a traditional role which had been emptied of viable political content by long years of dormancy. All of these tragically ambivalent figures had to innovate behavior that fulfilled the expectations of a frenzied mob, and in the end seem to have themselves gotten sufficiently caught up in the millenarian ferment which captured them to attempt sincerely to do just that.

VI

The 1857 uprising failed, as it had to fail, because it was the desperate, flailing attempt of a beleaguered cultural world to save itself from extinction. It was a noble fantasy; but, like all fantasies, it was doomed to evaporate before the remorseless power of contemporary technological reality mobilized in the service of the modern world's most rapidly ascending imperialist star. That it was primarily a revitalization movement and neither a grand conspiracy nor a war of national independence (although elements of both things were admittedly present in rudimentary degrees) cannot be seriously denied, it seems to me. Yet the uprising had traits which distinguish it from the revitalization movements recorded among primitive societies, and for this reason it needs to be seen as a particular type of this general class of social phenomena.

The chief basis for the differences between the 1857 uprising in India and, say, the Ghost Dance movement among the Indians of the Western plains lay precisely in the fact that India was not a primitive society, or series of them, as the case may be, but a highly complex civilization with cultural institutions of great antiquity and sophistication. Revitalization movements are ultimately political in nature; they are attempts to utilize the cultural resources of a people to *mobilize them for action,* designed to save the society and its culture from a perceived threat of disintegration and destruction emanating (usually) from an alien society. The forms that such movements take, therefore, are profoundly dependent upon the nature of the cultural and physical resources available to provide a basis for the mobilization process. Revitalization movements will be more bizarre the less the cultural world to be mobilized possesses institutional precedents for the kind of social structures needed to deal with the adversary at hand.

I regard this latter point as highly important in understanding the differences between revitalization movements in simpler and more complex societies, respectively. Earlier students of such movements failed to stress their political mobilizational aspects sufficiently and, especially in Wallace's case, laid one-sided emphasis on their psychological, culturological, and eschatological aspects. The latter are assuredly important, since they determine the symbolic structure and individual gratificatory potentialities of a given movement, but experience shows that these aspects continually undergo modification in accordance with its *political* fortunes. The Hindu-Muslim rapprochements which were born in the crisis of confrontation with the British, and which were ratified in symbolically universalistic cultural constructions like cow protection, would probably not have endured beyond that period of crisis confrontation had the rebels successfully blocked a British return. Their primary impetus was political mobilization.

With these general observations in mind, let me list a few of the features which I regard as being important and worthy of deeper investigation in the study of revitalistic movements of all kinds.

1. Revitalization processes are not confined to the simpler societies alone, where anthropologists developed their analytical orientation to them. They occur wherever social disorganization and social stress occur to such a degree that a sense of *cultural* deterioration, disintegration, or disaster pervades a whole society or a major segment of it. In India, the sepoys were a distillation of the sense of cultural doom pervading the entire Gangetic belt of peoples and became the organizational locus of their millenarian fantasies and craving for a reconstructed cultural system.

2. The context of revitalization movements is invariably a confrontation between societies that are *radically* disparate in technology, economy, and other ingredients of collective power. So-called "imperialist" situations are the most typical contemporary manifestations; here dominance and submission are rooted literally in differences in levels of technological evolution. Exploitation, the expropriation of resources, and the general instrumental manipulation of the subjugated society which results generate a cultural crisis and a revitalistic mobilization designed to resolve it. As the East India Company's power grew, England was moving into the Industrial Revolution and toward becoming a society pervasively dominated by economic rationality. Although herself a complex society, India was technologically less evolved than England and soon found her social structure and cultural system being radically manipulated to facilitate their

more rational integration into the administrative, economic, and even moral-ethical fabric of the Empire.

3. The reaction to domination and instrumental manipulation is an attempted political mobilization of the society's cultural resources. Achieving this requires emphasis on the separateness and the viability of the native culture as opposed to the "adversary" culture which has "invaded," diluted, and threatened to dissolve its victim unless disengagement and reactivation can be achieved. The requirement is met at the social level by heightening the sense of ethnic identity and pride and at the cultural level by stressing symbols, values, and eschatological belief systems which reject and oppose those of the aggressing society. Repeatedly, the mutineers in 1857 pointedly revived and restored customs and traditions which the British were known to abhor. Even the savage physical assaults upon and frequent mutilations of disarmed British civilians were symbolic statements of the extent to which irrevocable separation of the peoples, as well as of their cultures, was felt to be a necessary part of the regeneration process. A not dissimilar "ethnicization process" may be seen at work among a number of emerging peoples today, including, of course, the American Negro. At the cultural level, Eliade has identified the separation and opposition process at work in the cosmic regeneration myths that are an important feature of Melanesian cargo cults. Speaking of such a myth in the Markham valley, in which Satan was touted as the Supreme Being, he declares, "it is remarkable that Marafi (a particular prophet) had drawn the logical conclusion of an inevitable revolt against the religious and political usurpation of the Whites: the true god of the prophetic religion had to be the anti-God of the Whites, Satan."[14]

4. Revitalization movements rely heavily on religious values and belief systems because these are the most universally oriented

[14] Mircea Eliade, " 'Cargo Cults' and Cosmic Regeneration," *Millennial Dreams in Action*, ed. Sylvia L. Thrupp (New York: Schocken, 1970).

and the most obvious sources of ideological formulations capable of mobilizing supporters on an ethnic basis. Revitalistic leaders often have no political organizational precedents to draw upon, particularly if it is a case of a primitive society facing an industrialized society, with the result that they must innovate an organizational formula out of the meager cultural materials available to them. The religious system alone is usually the repository of such materials, since the requirement is for symbols and ideologies capable of generating widespread cohesion and concerted action against a tangible, better-organized adversary.

There were political organizational principles, as well as a rich reservoir of religious material, in the Indian experiential environment; but, as we saw, the trouble is that the political system was relevant to an earlier level of technological integration and, further, was severely atrophied after decades of dormancy. The rebels did, however, endeavor to utilize as best they could the old political principles in their attempted cultural reconstruction. Their approach to the establishment of the millennium differed from primitive nativism in precisely this respect, in fact, and that is the reason why it should be regarded as a type of revitalization movement characteristic of the confrontation between an industrial society and a complex, non-industrial society. The 1857 uprising did not turn to bizarre religious prophets who promised societies composed of resurrected ancestors cohabiting with corporeal man on an earth transformed into the Garden of Eden. Theirs was rather a *religiously pervaded prophecy* of a revitalized society governed by genuinely political figures, the deposed princes, whom they would restore to their past eminence after purging India of the contamination the hated *firingi* had inflicted upon it. A similar pattern emerged in China at about the same time as the 1857 uprising which historians call the Taiping rebellion. In both instances, and in others like them, their instigators could reach back into their own historical past and blend millenarian religion with well-developed political forms, because their rich and complex cultures contained these organizational precedents as available cultural resources. This is why the Indian uprising could look like a grand conspiracy of the princes and the sepoys to British historians and a patriotic war of independence to nationalist Indian historians when, in fact, it was neither. For neither party grasped the point that the princes, in other words, the symbols of traditional political authority, had been peremptorily co-opted by a frenzied melange of sepoys and peasants bent upon the utopianistic purification and reconstruction of Indian culture. As concrete individuals, the princes were almost incidental to the sepoys; so much so, in fact, that the sepoys would have shown little compunction about killing them had they been unwilling to play their necessary role in the unfolding cultural fantasy.

6. *Utopianism in Latin American Cultures*

JOSEPH L. LOVE
University of Illinois, Urbana

I

Utopianism as an attempt to construct an idealized and rational communitarian society is a phenomenon almost totally lacking in Latin America. During the nearly 500 years of colonial and national history in the region, one is hard pressed to find such movements, even during their nineteenth-century high tide in the United States and Europe. The lack of utopian movements *stricto sensu* requires us to focus principally on religious communitarianism and millenarianism, "folk" movements rather than rational social experiments.

The absence of utopianism nonetheless raises this interesting question: Why have utopian thought and action been so negligible in Latin America: In this short paper, only the briefest list of factors can be suggested: the existence of latifundium-based societies with many of the members of lower strata outside Western culture; the small size of a middle-class intelligentsia; the absence (until recently) of social stresses produced by industrialization; the course of Latin American political history, in which the problems of anarchy and tyranny absorbed the energies of the region's intellectuals; and perhaps a Luso-Hispanic "frame of mind," favoring doctrines in which social problems are placed in a cosmic frame of reference and for which utopian communities seem irrelevant—e.g., Thomism, Comtian positivism, and Marxism.

To be sure, there have been instances of utopian experiments as far back as the Spanish conquest. In the Indian communities under their supervision, Bartolomé de las Casas and Vasco de Quiroga tried to prove to the Spanish Crown that "Indians could live like Christian Spaniards."[1] In the seventeenth century, Jesuit missionaries in the Amazon valley and Paraguay organized utopian-like communities of their native charges in the famous "reductions," though here (as before) the Indians were treated as children, not as participants in an adult community.

Passing quickly to the nineteenth century, the classic age of Western utopianism, we may note the interesting fact that European utopian theorists were not ignored in Latin America; Saint-Simon and his successors had a sizeable impact, especially in the Rio de la Plata area. Esteban Echeverría and his fellow members of the Argentine Generation of 1837 adapted Saint-Simon's ideas to national problems—particularly the organization of a liberal nation-state. They thought they could engineer change from above. In Spanish America, "utopianism" in the first half of the

[1] Lewis Hanke, *The Spanish Struggle for Justice in the Conquest of America* (Philadelphia: University of Pennsylvania Press, 1949), Chs. 4, 5.

nineteenth century might even be equated with constitution writing; before 1850 it was generally assumed throughout the region that tyranny or the alternative evil of anarchy could be prevented by drafting a more perfect fundamental law.

In the latter part of the nineteenth century, something approximating a utopian movement appeared in Latin America. This was anarchism, and more precisely the anarchism of Bakunin and Malatesta. It was only in Spain itself, however, that this doctrine was associated with communitarianism, and there only in Andalusia, a region where the intellectual apparatus of anarchism was feebly developed. Andalusian anarchists were, by and large, secularized millenarians who believed the evils of the world could be exorcised forthwith through a cataclysmic event such as the massacre of the owners of local latifundia.[2] This "here and now" mentality, as Karl Mannheim called it, had its repercussions in Latin America as Spanish (and Italian) anarchists immigrated to Cuba, Argentina, Uruguay, and Brazil toward the end of the nineteenth century.

Anarchism generally gave way to communism among radical workers in the 1920's, but its "here and now" mentality ultimately seems to have found an heir in Fidel Castro's 26th of July movement. Before 1959, revolutionary action by Castro, and guerrilla warfare in particular, were aimed at bringing down a corrupt political and social system that "could not wait" for the rise of internal contradictions foreseen in orthodox Marxism. Not surprisingly, Cuban communists were still deriding the 26th of July as an exercise in political romanticism less than a year before Castro took power. Was it mere chance that Castro chose for this movement the red and black colors of anarchism? After his march into Havana in January, 1959, most of the liberal and

[2] E. J. Hobsbawm, *Primitive Rebels: Studies in Archaic Forms of Social Movements in the 19th and 20th Centuries,* 2d ed[?] (New York: Norton, 1965), Ch. 5.

libertarian ideas expressed in his speech *History Will Absolve Me* (1953) and later programs were abandoned to secure the consolidation of the new regime. Yet an element of the old mentality remained. Castro was in a hurry, and his socialist planning tended to become utopianism as the time allowed for fundamental change approached zero. For instance, he would have nothing of "five-year plans." Castro needed only a year to revolutionize Cuban agriculture. The year of agrarian reform (1960) was followed by the year of education, in which all illiterates in Cuba were to learn to read; next came the year of "planning."

I I

By the very examples I have chosen, it should be apparent that communal utopianism has no direct counterpart in Latin America. What is much more important is religious communitarianism.

Such movements have occurred in widely scattered areas of Latin America, but Brazil has probably had more than other countries. Brazil is also the Latin American nation in which millenarian and messianic communities have been most thoroughly studied, and there is a large literature in Portuguese, English, and French.[3] Most of these studies center on the social and economic

---

[3] Major studies include: Maria Isaura Pereira de Queiroz, *O messianismo no Brasil e no mundo* (São Paulo: Editôra da Universidade de São Paulo, 1965), and *Réforme et révolution dans les sociétés traditionelles: Histoire et ethnologie des mouvements messianiques* (Paris: Anthropos, 1968); Euclides da Cunha, *Rebellion in the Backlands*, trans. Samuel Putnam (Chicago: University of Chicago Press, 1944); Rui Facó, *Cangaceiros e fanáticos: Gênese e lutas* (Rio de Janeiro: Editôra Civilização Brasileira, 1963); Maurício Vinhas de Queiroz, *Messianismo e conflito social (A guerra sertaneja do Contestado; 1912–1916)* (Rio de Janeiro: Editôra Civilização Brasileira, 1966); René Ribeiro, "Brazilian Messianic Movements," *Comparative Studies in Society and History*, Suppl. 2 (1962):55–69; Ralph della Cava, "Brazilian Messianism and National

conditions which give rise to millenarianism, and much of the analysis is from a Marxist perspective. Broadly speaking, the scholarship to date has de-emphasized the specific developments of the various cults, the content of their creeds, and the particular historical circumstances in which the movements arose; in fact, the literature tends to be somewhat deterministic, since socio-economic conditions are often seen as the causal factors.[4] Yet until more detailed case studies appear, the "social" approach is a big advance over notions of racial and cultural primitivism which dominated contemporary analysis fifty years ago.

An interesting fact about the dozen or more sects and subsects that have appeared in Brazil is that they have almost all occurred in the nineteenth and twentieth centuries. The clustering of these groups in the national period (during which Brazil has changed at a far faster rate than in the colonial era) appears to substantiate the hypothesis of Eric J. Hobsbawm that such movements are reactions to modernization, and particularly to changes in land tenure and fiscal-legal structures of incipient capitalism.[5] In Brazil, the bulk of the movements not only took place in "modern" times, but specifically between 1889 and 1930, as secularization, urbanization, and new financial and legal practices threatened ancient social structures for the first time.

Their modern appearance notwithstanding, one of the characteristic themes of Brazilian messianism and millenarianism goes back to the sixteenth century—namely, the cult of King Sebas-

---

Institutions: A Reappraisal of Canudos and Joaseiro," *Hispanic American Historical Review* 48 (1968): 402–20; and *Miracle at Joaseiro* (New York: Columbia University Press, 1970). The studies by Pereira de Queiroz and by della Cava contain extensive bibliographies.

[4] Important exceptions (in the modern literature) which take into account historically unique circumstances and the specific features of their subjects' creeds are the works by Vinhas de Queiroz and by della Cava, cited in n. 3.

[5] Hobsbawm, *Primitive Rebels*, pp. 1–3.

tian. This crusading monarch of Portugal had the misfortune to die childless in a battle against the Moors in 1578, after which Philip II of Spain claimed the Portuguese crown for his own. In the years of Portugal's "Babylonian Captivity" to the kings of Castile (1580–1640), a messianic cult arose among the Portuguese peasantry which affirmed that Sebastian would miraculously return to Portugal and drive out the hated Spaniards. As Portuguese colonists drifted into colonial Brazil, "Sebastianism" came with them, and the movement easily survived the ouster of the Spanish from Lisbon in 1640. In Brazil, European travelers commented on the existence of the Sebastianist sect in the early nineteenth century, but its most famous manifestation occurred after Brazil had shifted from monarchy to republic in 1889. Seven years after the proclamation of the republic, a rebellion broke out in the backlands of Bahia State against the "wicked" republic. Its leader was a man called Antônio Conselheiro (Anthony the Counsellor), a lay mystic who set up a community at Canudos, Bahia, and preached the return of Sebastian and the end of the world at the turn of the century. Conselheiro condemned the republic for separating church and state, and he had become particularly incensed at a local tax which he correctly attributed to the new political and fiscal system. Therefore, the movement was in part a reaction to the development of a modern secular state.

In the initial years of the republic, Bahian politicians not only tolerated the sect and its communistic tendencies but manipulated it for its economic and political potential.[6] Ultimately, Conselheiro fell afoul of state and then national authorities, and federal troops marched on Canudos to destroy the village. To the surprise of "civilized" Brazil, however, a few thousand poorly armed Sebastianists defeated three military expeditions

---

[6] della Cava, "Brazilian Messianism," p. 411.

in a brilliant display of guerrilla tactics. Only a fourth campaign involving almost a third of the Brazilian army was able to defeat the rebels, annihilating Canudos and its inhabitants. The epic story of how the followers of Antônio Conselheiro lived and died was set down by Euclides da Cunha, a witness to the campaign and one of Brazil's greatest writers. His account of the Canudos affair, *Os Sertões* (translated as *Rebellion in the Backlands*), is regarded by many Brazilians as the single most important book about their country.

But Canudos was not the only messianic movement of its era. Half a dozen cults—several of them Sebastianist—erupted in widely scattered areas of the Brazilian backlands between 1889 and 1930, in which year Getúlio Vargas's revolution initiated a new phase of modernization. After 1930, millenarianism and messianism declined, though they by no means disappeared.[7] The rise of secular forms of protest in the countryside, the penetration of roads and cheap bus transportation into the interior of Brazil to permit emigration, and the increasing power of the state to alleviate the misery of natural disasters and to contain violent protest through military means—these were the factors which caused the decline of peasant religious movements. Thus, as Brazil has moved further along the road of modernization, millenarian and messianic outbreaks have tended to disappear, though their high tide had occurred during the initial stages of change.

III

The conclusion would be unwarranted, however, that economically developed countries are exempted from messianic and millenarian movements. In fact, such a group of "primitive rebels" (as Hobsbawm generically styles peasants reacting to mod-

[7] Ribeiro, "Brazilian Messianic Movements," pp. 68–69.

ernization) exists today in the United States. This unexpected development and the ways in which the movement is received in a modern society are the subject of the remainder of this paper. The theme is still Hispanic messianism and millenarianism, for the rebels in question are members of the Alianza Federal de Mercedes (Federal Alliance of Land Grants) with headquarters in Albuquerque, New Mexico. The organization attained notoriety on a national scale in June, 1967, when its militants seized the courthouse in the town of Tierra Amarilla (northwest of Santa Fe). Simultaneously they set up a *pueblo-república*, a city-state, which they asserted was completely independent of the United States and the state of New Mexico. To put down the revolt, the governor of New Mexico called in the National Guard and created a sensation by fielding armored tanks and corralling suspected rebels and their families into detention camps.

What occurred at Tierra Amarilla and threatens to erupt again occurred in a "modern" society, to be sure, but the national perspective is necessarily deceptive. The Hispanic culture of New Mexico, which dates from the early seventeenth century, has been both conservative and (to a certain extent) resilient. The disintegration of this culture along the tributaries of the upper Rio Grande is in fact a contemporary phenomenon, and the rise of the Alianza is in part a form of resistance to anomie.

In my opinion, the Alianza rebellion must be understood at two levels—that of the national society with its modern social relations and technology, and that of the local situation which gave the movement its peculiar features. At the national level, the rise of the Alianza in New Mexico coincided with the appearance of Mexican-American movements from Texas to California in the 1960's. Reformist groups such as the Mexican-American Political Association (MAPA) and the United Farm Workers' Organizing Committee (UFWOC), as well as radical groups like the Brown Berets of Los Angeles (the Mexican-American equivalent of the Black Panthers), are products of the 1960's—as is the Alianza. Nor were the Mexican-Americans a negligible minority group. In the 1960 census, they accounted for 12 percent of the population in the southwestern states of Texas, New Mexico, Arizona, Colorado, and California—about three and a half million people.[8]

Yet in New Mexico, the culture of Hispanos (the local equivalent of Mexican-Americans) is something distinct from its counterparts in California and Texas, where 80 percent of the Southwest's Mexican-Americans live. In the latter two states, the Latin populations principally consist of persons who crossed the border after 1900 or have descended from those who did. In New Mexico, by contrast, some elements of the population go back to the founding of Santa Fe in 1609; few persons in the Hispano-populated counties along the upper Rio Grande have any memory of connections with Mexico. As in California and Texas, the population is largely mestizo; but the New Mexican Hispanos make a point of distinguishing themselves from the "Mexicans," those newcomers who entered the United States in this century.

Space does not permit a description of the slow erosion of Hispano power in New Mexico following the U.S. takeover in 1848, but a central feature of this process was the Anglo-Americans' legal and extra-legal wresting of lands from the Hispanos. The shift to Anglo power has accelerated since World War II. In the decade 1950–60, the Anglo population rose 59 percent, while the Hispano element increased only 8 percent. By 1960, Anglo-Americans comprised about two-thirds of the state's population, and New Mexico had the highest rate of male unemployment among its Mexican-American population of the

[8] Donald N. Barrett, "Demographic Characteristics," in Julian Samora, ed., *La Raza: Forgotten Americans* (Notre Dame, Ind.: Notre Dame University Press, 1966), p. 160.

five southwestern states in 1960. In that census year, 10.3 percent of the Hispano males were unemployed, and lack of work was a major problem in both urban and rural areas.[9] Urbanization itself was creating serious problems of adjustment and threatening traditional family relationships. In 1965, for instance, one investigator found that eight-ninths of the women receiving aid for dependent children in Bernalillo County (location of Albuquerque) had Spanish surnames.[10]

In the countryside, as well, the old ways have been disappearing. Pastoralism (sheep-herding in particular) has been a favorite way of life on the upper Rio Grande and its tributaries since the 1600's, but in this century corporations have gobbled up individual holdings and forced Hispanos into other pursuits. Corporate ownership has also had the effect of disrupting the *patrón-pastor* (patriarchal landlord–shepherd) relationship so characteristic of traditional Hispanic society. Until recently, Hispano pastoralists sought refuge in the use of federally owned lands, where grazing privileges were allowed before droughts induced the Forest Service to cut back sharply on this practice.

The area where the Alianza Federal de Mercedes has had the biggest impact is in Tierra Amarilla and surrounding Rio Arriba County, just south of the Colorado line. In Rio Arriba, per capita income in 1967 was less than $1,000 per year, and 11,000 of the 23,000 residents of the county were on welfare roles in 1967. In the 1960 census the county had the state's highest rate of unemployment—15.1 percent, a figure almost three times the state average.

[9] Ibid., pp. 161, 189.

[10] Nancie L. González, *The Spanish Americans of New Mexico: A Distinctive Heritage* (Los Angeles: Mexican-American Study Project, University of California, Los Angeles, 1967), p. 92. Unfortunately, this figure includes an unknown number of non-Hispano Mexican-Americans who had immigrated to Albuquerque from Texas. The same problem arises with other aggregate data (e.g., the population figures mentioned above) which rely solely on Spanish surnames and omit place of birth.

The near-desperate situation of Rio Arriba and other Hispano-populated counties of northern New Mexico was the milieu in which the Alianza appeared in 1963 and soon began to thrive. The central purpose of the Alianza is to reclaim lands taken from the Hispanos over the last century; in all, it claims 3.7 million acres in the Southwest, but its leaders would settle as a start for the 500,000 acres in Kit Carson Forest, which includes most of Rio Arriba County. The legal basis for such a demand is derived from the *Recopilación de leyes de los reinos de Indias*, generally known in English as *The Laws of the Indies*. This celebrated compilation of Spanish colonial law was drawn up in 1681 and stated, among other things, that the common property of towns and villages could not be alienated. Rural properties of the villages were called *ejidos* and are of special interest to the Alianza. The villagers who subscribe to Alianza doctrines want to recuperate common lands lost after the Treaty of Guadalupe Hidalgo ended the war between the United States and Mexico in 1848; they long to engage again in their traditional occupation, sheep-herding.[11] The Alianza moreover asserts that *The Laws of the Indies* granted the *pueblos* (a word meaning "towns," "peoples," "communities") near-complete autonomy, and its members transliterate the seventeenth-century word *república* as "republic." Thus the pueblos-repúblicas are "free city-states." That *The Laws of the Indies* have been superseded by Mexican law in 1821 or U.S. law in 1848, the Alianza flatly denies. Thus we might classify the Aliancistas as utopians in one sense, as they await the return of a golden age.

This movement now claims 30,000 members, though one student of the organization (González) has estimated 10,000 as a more accurate figure. But there may well be 20,000 more sympathizers beyond the regular dues-payers. That the Alianza

[11] Ibid., p. 35.

could develop so rapidly since its founding in 1963 is above all a tribute to the charisma and organizing ability of the movement's president, Reies López Tijerina. Tijerina is not a New Mexican by birth, curiously enough, but a Mexican-American born in south Texas. He is a spellbinding orator with a taste for violent rhetoric and gesticulations. As a youth, he wandered across the Southwest picking seasonal crops, and he later became a preacher in the Assembly of God church, a fact which added a stock of Pentecostal metaphors to his speeches. In the 1950's his career consisted of preaching and picking crops in Texas, Illinois, Michigan, Arizona, and New Mexico. Tijerina therefore had a much broader picture of the Mexican-American community than did the relatively stationary and pastorally oriented Hispanos of rural New Mexico. In 1960 Tijerina settled in New Mexico and subsequently married into Hispano society. In the early 1960's he also made the acquaintance of another "outsider," an Anglo-American named Gerry Noll, who apparently provided him with the land-grants doctrine of *The Laws of the Indies*. On the basis that ancient body of law, Tijerina set up the Alianza Federal de Mercedes, and he later traveled to both Mexico and Spain in search of legal evidence for his case.

Yet the legal path was thorny and inevitably full of frustrations. In American courts the Alianza's legal arguments were dismissed out of hand, and the general course of Alianza activity moved from attempted litigation to direct (and violent) action. As early as 1964, Tijerina's followers had engaged in a brief skirmish to seize federal lands in Rio Arriba County; but as long as Tijerina was seeking legal redress and firing off protests to various state and federal agencies, the movement was largely non-violent. In October, 1966, a second incident occurred, in which the Aliancistas "arrested" a pair of rangers in the Carson Forest and proclaimed the existence of the Republic of San Joaquín del Chama. Almost immediately the leaders were rounded up, and Tijerina and his lieutenants were charged with commandeering government property (a federally owned truck) and assaulting forest rangers.

In the meantime, Tijerina, Noll, and others charged in the 1966 affair were out on bond (pending appeal), and in June, 1967, the third and most publicized flare-up occurred at the Tierra Amarilla courthouse. This time the rebels allegedly shot the deputy sheriff, bombed the courthouse, and made a hostage of a newspaper reporter assigned to cover the event. State troopers and the New Mexico National Guard dispersed the attackers, and four days after the raid Tijerina was again under arrest. He and other Alianza militants were charged with kidnapping, attempted murder, and bombing a public building. Yet only a few weeks later, Tijerina was free on bail once more, and he began to crisscross the nation in search of support. In September and October, he appeared at the National Conference for New Politics in Chicago, spoke at a rally in Los Angeles against U.S. involvement in Viet Nam, and made Labor Day speeches to Mexican-American groups in San Antonio and Austin, Texas. He seemed willing to ally with almost any group with grievances against the "system," seeking the friendship of Elijah Muhammad's Black Muslims, the Black Panthers, SNCC, and the Brown Berets, as well as the more "respectable" MAPA and UFWOC.

Parallel to Tijerina's attempt to garner support from modern radical and reformist groups at the national level came a quite different development in the Alianza itself—the rise of millenarian visions[12] among the "parochial" grass-roots constituency on the upper Rio Grande and its tributaries. According to some of the Aliancistas,[13] a miracle took place during the Kit Carson

---

[12] The millenarian element of the movement was first noted in ibid., pp. 71–72.

[13] Interviews with Gerry Noll and others, Albuquerque, N.M., September 10, 1967.

invasion in 1966 and again at the Tierra Amarilla battle in 1967. On both occasions a double rainbow appeared in the sky, a sign that God approved of the actions the Aliancistas were taking. It also symbolized the fact that Montezuma, of whom Reies Tijerina was the prophet, would soon return to New Mexico and drive out or destroy the hated Anglo usurpers. The rationale of the coming millennium is something like this: The annexation of New Mexico by the United States in 1848 and the collusion of upper-class Hispanos with the so-called Santa Fe Ring constituted a fall from grace. Ancient property rights were abrogated, and the Hispano lower classes (*el pueblo*) were placed in a state of subjugation. They must remain in darkness and degradation until Montezuma returns to punish the Anglo aggressors and their traitorous Hispano collaborators. Tijerina is Montezuma's precursor.

The religious history of the Hispanic folk of the upper Rio Grande probably contributed to this millenarian outburst. A secret Catholic lay brotherhood of flagellants and mystics called the Penitentes has existed in this area of New Mexico for centuries and has received considerable attention from both anthropologists and writers of tourist guidebooks. What is less well known—or remembered—is the fact that the Hispano towns of the upper Rio Grande region were foci of Pentecostal revivalism in the 1930's. An observer in 1937 noted that "passages from the Revelation of St. John are favorite texts, and lead to frenzies of religious ecstasy." The same writer thought that as many as one-half the inhabitants of many Hispano towns had joined this sect, called the Allelujahs.[14] Though the movement apparently subsided in the 1940's and 1950's, the fact that Tijerina was a former Pentecostal minister probably aided the release of millenarian hopes, especially after the Forest Service curtailed grazing rights.

[14] John B. Johnson, "The Allelujahs: A Religious Cult in Northern New Mexico," *Southwest Review* 22 (1937):132–33.

In October, 1967, the millenarian and messianic elements produced a weird by-product, as a convention of the Alianza decided to transform Tijerina's assistant Gerry Noll into the "King of the Indies." Noll now became Don Barne Quinto César, the direct descendant of Ferdinand VII of Spain, the King of the Indies at the time of Mexican independence. In a legal notice in an Albuquerque newspaper, Noll had written a few months earlier:

> . . . KNOW YE that We have exclusive and supreme jurisdiction within [New Mexico] over all persons and property situated therein. . . .
>
> WE cannot afford to permit the present status quo to be maintained without actually destroying Our independence and autonomy. Consequently, We must take measures calculated to curtail the activities of any aggressors with the utmost dispatch. We shall enter troops in these territories to restore Our authority . . . woe to him who obeys the orders of the aggressor, for he shall be punished without mercy. . . .
>
> THEREFORE KNOW YE that We shall commence to liberate Our kingdoms, realms, and dominions. . . . We shall not take any prisoners of war, but shall take only war criminals and traitors and try [them] by a military tribunal and execute them [*Albuquerque Journal*, Feb. 20, 1967].

Were this assertion that of an isolated individual, it would have little import; but Tijerina arranged for the general convention to accept Noll's dynastic claim by a unanimous vote.

In November, a month after the Alianza convention, the trials stemming from the 1966 incident began, and testimony revealed the colorful facts that Noll's real name was Gerald Wayne Barnes (origin of Don Barne?) and that he had been convicted of bank robbery in 1945, grand larceny in 1949, forgery in 1953, and third-degree assault in 1963. At the end of the trial (in which he was given a three-year term), Noll defied the court's authority and remained unperturbed by the whole affair. "I am willing to die for my country and my people. This is part of my job as king and all in a day's work," he declared. In the same proceedings, Tijerina received a two-year sentence, but both he and Noll were soon out on bond again. In January, the deputy sheriff in Tierra Amarilla was murdered, and Tijerina and his principal aides were once more brought into custody. In the next few months they were repeatedly in and out of jail.

Since that time, legal troubles have kept the Alianza leaders busy, and Tijerina has only occasionally surfaced at the national level, most prominently for an appearance at the Poor People's March on Washington in May, 1968. Quarreling with the black leadership, Tijerina would not let his followers join the campers in Resurrection City. Instead he took advantage of his presence in Washington to lecture State Department officials on the Treaty of Guadalupe Hidalgo, which required the United States to respect Mexican property rights (including existing *ejidos*). In November the Tierra Amarilla trial commenced, during which Tijerina suddenly dismissed his legal counsel and undertook his own defense. In mid-December his self-assurance was rewarded by an acquittal on the most serious charges, including kidnapping. But other charges stemming from the events of 1966 and 1967, plus new ones, continued to plague Tijerina. In October, 1969, he was convicted of aiding in the destruction of a Forest Service sign and assaulting a Forest Service agent the previous June, and received a three-year term. A few days later the U.S. Supreme Court refused to review the conviction on 1966 charges. Finally, in November, 1969, the Alianza leader was convicted of false imprisonment and assault with intent to commit a felony at Tierra Amarilla in 1967; as a result, he was sentenced to concurrent terms of one to five years and two to ten years at the beginning of 1970.

Tijerina still clings to his single issue—obtaining the lost land grants—rather than modifying his program toward reformist ends or a more conventionally radical stance. The situation in 1970 was still plastic, and if Tijerina remains in prison, the Alianza might even disappear in the wake of a more modern movement, reformist or radical. In any case, Yonina Talmon's observation that millenarian movements form a connecting link between pre-political and modern political organizations seems an appropriate way to look at the Alianza Federal de Mercedes.[15]

Yet the rise of this movement in a modern economy and society has had consequences different from those in countries undergoing the initial stresses of modernization, such as Brazil between 1889 and 1930. (Indeed, the very appearance of the Alianza was probably related to the political mobilization of Mexican-Americans throughout the Southwest.) González has emphasized the revitalization element (as defined by Anthony Wallace) in the Alianza, while Swadesh has denied the validity of this approach because of the innovating elements and national connections of the organization.[16]

I believe the problem here is the failure to see two distinct dimensions of the movement, one which we can associate with

---

[15] Yonina Talmon, "Pursuit of the Millennium: The Relation between Religious and Social Change," *Archives Européenes de Sociologie* 3 (1962):141–43.

[16] González, *The Spanish Americans of New Mexico: A Distinctive Heritage*, p. 68. Frances L. Swadesh, "The Alianza Movement: Catalyst for Social Change in New Mexico," in June Helm, ed., *Spanish-Speaking People in the United States: Proceedings of the 1968 Annual Spring Meeting of the American Ethnological Society* (Seattle: University of Washington Press, 1968), esp. p. 174. Other studies dealing specifically with the Alianza are Joseph L. Love, "La Raza: Mexican-Americans in Rebellion," in *Trans-action: Social Science and Modern Society* 6, No. 4 (February, 1969):35–41; Peter Nabokov, *Tijerina and the Courthouse Raid* (Albuquerque: University of New Mexico Press, 1969); and Richard Gardner, *¡Grito! Reies Tijerina and the New Mexico Land Grant War of 1967* (Indianapolis: Bobbs-Merrill, 1970). The latter two works are chronicles by perceptive journalists.

the rural, "primitive," society of the upper Rio Grande and the other with urban, "modern," nationally integrated Albuquerque, where Alianza headquarters are located. The "visible," media-oriented sector is modern, but the "invisible," millenarian sector is not. Links with MAPA or the Brown Berets mean little to Tijerina's grass-roots supporters on the upper Rio Grande. But the urban sector, identified primarily with the leadership, is not just sham; the advanced capitalist society in which this "primitive rebellion" appeared necessarily adds a modern dimension and creates an inner tension in the Alianza.

7. Utopian Communities and Social Networks

GEORGE L. HICKS
Brown University

I

Whether utopianism—the desire to create an ideal situation in this world—is confined to the European cultural tradition, as some scholars insist,[1] or not, the attempt to establish utopian communities has been a persistent feature in the history of the

Field data for this essay were collected, with the assistance of Linné H. Hicks, in Banner community from June, 1965, to August, 1966. The field research was supported by a Pre-Doctoral Fellowship from the Social Science Research Council. I am grateful for the critical comments of Niels W. Braroe and Philip E. Leis, who read an earlier draft of these paragraphs.

[1] Ernest Tuveson, "The Power of Believing," *Comparative Studies in Society and History* 5 (1963):466–77.

United States. Before the Civil War, 130 of these settlements had been started in this country.[2] Indeed the colonial period, in the elaborate plans for the royal colony of Georgia no less than in the Puritans' goal of making the New Jerusalem in Massachusetts Bay, was heavily colored with utopian ideals.[3] "Let us begin anew," an essential part of utopian programs, is, even today, a recurrent theme in the national political rhetoric.

In light of the ease with which the American social experience can be regarded as "The Quest for Paradise,"[4] the fact that utopian communities are still being built should not be surprising. A recent compilation includes forty such communities extant in 1967, with ten more in the process of formation.[5] There is a constant process of fusion and dissolution among them and a constant attempt to establish entirely new ones. While some of the "tribes" of the new bohemians—the hippies—might be considered utopian communities, they seem to lack one of the central aims of other American utopian efforts, past and present: that of setting an example for mankind. "Doing your own thing," as the hippies enjoin us, is an imperative far too hedonistic and self-consciously escapist for the taste of most residents in utopian communities. One federation of utopian or, as they prefer, *intentional* communities has stated its goal in this way: "Intentional community is an effort to create a social order which may in time become more universally accepted and so help to create the inclusive human community where the normal thing is to practice mutual concern, respect and love and to share cooperatively

[2] Arthur Bestor, *Backwoods Utopias: The Sectarian and Owenite Phases of Communitarian Socialism in America, 1663–1829* (Philadelphia: University of Pennsylvania Press, 1950), esp. pp. 235–42.

[3] Daniel Boorstin, *The Americans: The Colonial Experience* (New York: Random House, 1958), pp. 80–88.

[4] Charles L. Sanford, *The Quest for Paradise: Europe and the American Moral Imagination* (Urbana: University of Illinois Press, 1961).

[5] See *Directory of Social Change*, issued by *The Modern Utopian* (Medford, Mass., 1967).

and democratically in the responsibility, work and use of the values of life."[6]

At the base of most utopian enterprises lies the assumption, as Spiro has noted for the kibbutzim, that "raw human nature, if nourished in the 'proper' social environment, can give rise to that kind of human being who approximates, at least, man's noblest image of himself."[7] To establish the appropriate environment for the birth of this noble man, the utopian plan is to start on a small scale by building distinctive communities. Bestor takes this utopian goal of peaceful revolution by example as the focus of his description of nineteenth-century "communitarians," who believed that "a microcosm of society . . . could undergo drastic change in complete harmony and order, and the great world outside could be relied on to imitate a successful experiment without coercion or conflict."[8]

However necessary it might appear to utopian community-builders to withdraw from the larger society in order to create their alternative, actual secession is, of course, impossible. In most cases, full retreat is not desired, for utopians are ordinarily "more eager to reform [the] world than to resign from it, even when they flee to hinterlands where its importunings are weakest."[9] Their major problem is to adapt to the larger society's institutions without relinquishing their self-image as dissenting idealists.

But allaying the potentially hostile elements of the surrounding world is only part of a utopian community's adaptation. They must also solve the related problem of securing support of vari-

[6] Fellowship of Intentional Communities, *The Intentional Communities: 1959 Yearbook* (Yellow Springs, Ohio: Fellowship of Intentional Communities, 1959), p. 2.

[7] Melford Spiro, *Kibbutz: Venture in Utopia* (New York: Schocken Books, 1963), p. 3.

[8] Bestor, *Backwoods Utopias*, p. 4.

[9] David W. Plath, "The Fate of Utopia: Adaptive Tactics in Four Japanese Groups," *American Anthropologist* 68 (1966):1152.

ous kinds for what usually turn out to be fragile social experiments. It is this aspect of utopian communities that I am concerned with here. I hope to show that the relationships of one contemporary American utopia with its allies and sympathizers outside are crucial for the continued existence of the community. Both as channels for recruits and as channels for reassurances to the utopians that their efforts are unique and worthwhile, these links to the outside are indispensable.

II

Banner community—this, and the names I use for its members, are pseudonyms—a secular utopian experiment, spreads over 1,200 acres of forested land in the southern Appalachians. It was established in 1937 as a haven for youths who, in the words of its founder, "felt like social outcasts" from the urban industrial milieu of the United States. Charles Randolph, the community's founder and chairman of its initial three-man board of directors, was in de facto control of the project from the beginning. None of the directors has ever lived in the community, and even Randolph has spent only short periods of time there each year.

There seems to have been agreement among the directors that, as Randolph later put it, "life is too complex and too large to fit into any formal ideology." They expected Banner eventually to become economically self-supporting and politically self-governing. Yet they failed to specify either what political and economic structure the community should have or what kinds of persons should be accepted into it. In a letter to the community manager, hired to recruit members and temporarily oversee community activities, Randolph stated that those who were invited to join should be "persons and families . . . with strong commitment to building a sound life pattern . . . who wanted a chance to work out their own plans, living in simplicity and relative freedom. Given such traits, we [will] leave these people to work out personal, social and economic relationships as such persons normally would, doubtless learning much from their own experience." He did not, however, want to open the community to visionaries and escapists who sought utopian balm for personal ills. The project was to be conducted in a practical manner, an emphasis reflected in the choice of a 4-H club handicrafts counselor as the first manager.

Instructed to travel through the southern Appalachian region and find six or more families of "young men and women of such quality that they would add strength and character to the community," the manager took less than a month to fill the membership quota. Randolph recalls that on his next visit to Banner community, he "found settled on the land a group of men, not one of whom could have the slightest understanding of the purpose of the undertaking, and not one of whom was a person of more than very mediocre personality." They were impoverished farmers looking for shelter from the hardships of economic depression. Faced with the founder's lack of specificity in stating the criteria for membership, the manager, a man reared in the traditions of southern Appalachia, had to act on his own interpretation. From his point of view, those he had recruited *were* committed "to building a sound life pattern"; that they were poor, ill-educated, and not especially idealistic seemed to him irrelevant. He merely presented community membership to them in the same way he thought of his own managerial position: as a better economic opportunity. The new members and the manager stayed in Banner less than a year.

After other failures to attract community members of the proper caliber, Randolph turned for another manager to those groups he knew best: the various social-activist organizations of the Quakers.

Within a few months after the new man, a Quaker minister, took up residence in the community, the United States was involved in World War II. Most suitable prospects for Banner were liable for conscription, and the community grew very slowly during the wartime years. Members recruited in this period (1941–45), almost all of whom left shortly for Civilian Public Service camps as conscientious objectors, shared with the new manager certain beliefs not only about the aims and significance of Banner community but about other more general issues. They were pacifists; they longed to escape the conformity and commercialism of American society; they wanted to live in harmony with people like themselves. They conceived of Banner as an environment tolerant of individual eccentricities. Rather than viewing the community as a step in the improvement of a personal standard of living—as had been the strategy of previous settlers—they hoped to find refuge from a world they did not like and, at the same time, aid in the creation of new social forms. With few exceptions, recruits to Banner community since that time have arrived with similar perspectives.

After the war, the community rapidly filled with men released from prison or C.P.S. camps. News of Banner community, and an invitation to join it, had been spread by Randolph in his many visits to C.P.S. camps, and by the pacifist manager in articles written for Quaker magazines and at numerous activist conferences. By 1948, Banner community had become self-governing, with decisions made by the members invariably approved by the board of directors. The organization formed in those postwar years remains essentially unchanged.

III

In 1966, there were sixty-seven persons either resident in the community's twenty households or on temporary leaves of absence. Not all of them were enrolled members of the community, but almost every one of the twenty-nine adults participated in the monthly community meetings, where the group's major decisions are made. Committee meetings, work parties, and informal social activities provide numerous opportunities for the entire group to assemble at least once every two weeks. Occasions on which smaller numbers of residents come together arise almost daily.

Decisions in these various meetings are reached through consensus techniques, sometimes labeled by the members with a Quaker phrase, "sense of the meeting." The desire for a harmonious and unified membership is, in its political aspects, embodied in this method of reaching agreement. It serves to involve the total membership in each decision and to insure that, once a decision is taken, no disgruntled minority survives to weaken community solidarity. The goal is much the same as that recorded for Indian village *panchayats* by Bailey, and it appears to rest on the same ideological foundation: the belief that "conflict is not inevitable and a part of human nature: it is the product of wrong institutions."[10]

Community land is held in common, with real estate taxes assessed and paid on the entire tract jointly. Each member can be granted a plot of land under the terms of the organization's complicated land-holding agreement, which the members insist is neither lease nor deed but a unique instrument of land tenure. If a landholder leaves, he is guaranteed partial repayment for financial investments made in improving the holding. Few other communal projects now exist, although many attempts have been

[10] F. G. Bailey, "Decisions by Consensus in Councils and Committees: With Special Reference to Village and Local Government in India," in Michael Banton, ed., *Political Systems and the Distribution of Power*, Association of Social Anthropologists, Monograph 2 (London: Tavistock Publications, 1965), p. 4.

made to establish them. In the early 1950's, for example, several families formed a "common purse" arrangement for the pooling of wealth and labor. That experiment was cut short by the defection of most of those involved to the Society of Brothers, a modern Hutterian group.

Economic activities of the residents vary, with one or two persons employed in the local economy—as county librarian, for instance—and many of them making their living within the boundaries of the community itself. A medical clinic, operated by a physician who is a community member, draws most of its patients from the local population. One family owns a small pottery business, and another conducts a summer camp for urban children.

Most of Banner community's families are involved in the operation of a boarding school established in 1962. The school offers instruction in the junior high school grades and draws the greater part of its students from the outside. About half of the twenty-six pupils in the 1966–67 term were children from other utopian communities or from families engaged in radical pacifist activities. The remainder are the offspring of professional people, with a heavy representation of children from academic families. The school's staff is a combination of permanent community residents and of conscientious objectors who teach for two years of alternate service. Some persons on the "junior staff," all of whom are temporary employees, are college students who come to Banner to fulfill the requirements of work-study programs.

Three enterprises are operated by the school: a mail-order pharmaceutical business, a job-printing plant, and a used clothing store. These enterprises are considered as part of the educational program, rather than as purely profit-making ventures, and students work in all three. In addition, the school conducts a summer family camp with several one-week sessions each year. In the words of its promotional brochure, the school "is a unique education experiment. Working at the junior high school level, it approaches education not as preparation for life, but as life itself. It seeks to blend the academic, economic and social life of the school community into a single process."

Before enrolling, pupils in nearly every case have attended either the family camp or the children's camp, which is owned by a staff member. Adults who come to family camp often continue their association with the community through further visits and correspondence. They comprise part of the extensive network of relations which links Banner with its allies.

I V

One useful way of examining the relationships of Banner community's residents with a large number of persons outside is by applying the concept of social network. Elizabeth Bott's definition is succinct: "A network is a social configuration in which some, but not all, of the component external units maintain relationships with one another. The external units do not make up a larger social whole. They are not surrounded by a common boundary."[11] In considering how Banner community is linked with the "like-minded," I take "network" to be an inclusive term indicating the dispersed "social field" of groups and persons with whom community residents carry on relations of friendship and acquaintance.

The network of any particular resident overlaps with that of any other, so that a large number of the same persons outside the community are acquaintances of most residents. The significant segment of these overlapping networks, in the view of the uto-

[11] Elizabeth Bott, *Family and Social Network* (London: Tavistock Publications, 1957), pp. 216–17. See also J. A. Barnes, "Class and Committees in a Norwegian Island Parish," *Human Relations* 7 (1954):39–58.

pians, is made up of those who share the ideological perspectives of the residents. Some of these people belong to other utopian communities, but there are many who carry on radical political activities in other ways. Certain attitudes and interests are pervasive among those the utopians regard as "ideological comrades." Among these are a desire to bring about a non-violent social revolution and a tendency to over-estimate and dramatize the opposition to their efforts on the part of the larger society.

The ties of community residents and their outside acquaintances are sustained by personal visits and correspondence, circulation of specialized newsletters and magazines, and joint participation in conferences, peace marches, and public demonstrations for several causes. Residents contribute money to such pacifist organizations as the Fellowship of Reconciliation, Peacemakers, War Resisters' League, and the Committee for Non-Violent Action. A few serve on the editorial boards of the publications of these groups, and many of them attend conferences sponsored by pacifists. Articles describing Banner community appear in pacifist journals and in such utopian magazines as *A Way Out* and *The Modern Utopian*. Each summer, several of the community's many visitors come because they have learned of its existence from these publications.[12] Some visitors strengthen ties created with individual community residents on this initial trip by returning for participation in the summer camps or the school.

The extent of contact with other utopian settlements can be illustrated by the activities of Banner and its residents in aiding a besieged group in the Deep South. Koinonia, a tiny religious community in central Georgia, was for several years in the late 1950's under assault from its local neighbors, both through eco-

[12] *The Modern Utopian* recognizes its function as guidebook. See the remark in the October–November, 1967, issue (Vol. 2, No. 2), p. 32: "We plan to have the May–June [1968] issue distributed early in June in order to aid those planning to visit communities during the summer."

nomic reprisal and armed attack. The interracial nature of Koinonia, and especially its function as a headquarters for civil rights organizers in the area, was the focus of local displeasure. In this crisis, Banner community sent a small cash loan. Further, as a personal gesture of support, one woman from Banner went to Koinonia to assist in its mail-order cake and pecan business. While she was there, she insisted upon taking a turn as night watchman and was fired upon by a carload of local assailants. As she told the story: "There was actually little chance of being hit by a bullet and even if you are, you're not likely to be killed. Nevertheless, I decided not to alarm my family by telling them of the incident and didn't realize that Dorothy Day, who was with me, would write it up for the *Catholic Worker*. When my daughter found out by reading the *Worker*, she joked about it and said to me: 'You forgot that it's a small world, Mother!' "[13]

Both the community and the school attract short-term visitors who can conveniently be called "transient utopians." One such man has been to Banner twice in the past three years. Each time he has led discussions in the community's Quaker meeting, presented a short talk on pacifism and race relations to classes at the school, and stayed for a few weeks in a resident's household. He has lived in several utopian settlements—Toulome Farms in California, Koinonia and Macedonia in Georgia, the Society of Brothers in New York—but refuses to accept membership in any of them. Like Banner's residents, he is well acquainted with many people in the civil rights and peace movements all over the nation, and he joins with them at times on picket lines and marches. On his travels, this itinerant herald wears a sandwich board inscribed with slogans similar to the one he arrived with in Banner: "Jesus Taught Us to Love One Another / Try It."

In the conversations of visitors and residents, there are fre-

---

[13] On the *Catholic Worker*, see *Fellowship Magazine* 31, No. 9, (September 1965).

quent allusions to comrades with whom they have associated in prison or C.P.S. camps, in memorable peace vigils (e.g., the "Omaha Action" of 1955), and in former utopian communities (e.g., Kingwood community in New Jersey, 1948–53). They draw together bits of news and gossip about mutual acquaintances and relate anecdotes of previous adventures. Personal references are often made to a limited number of radical heroes: Martin Luther King, Staughton Lynd, Norman Morrison, A. J. Muste, and others.

V

With respect to recruitment, the community's situation is very much like that of many utopian groups in this country: there is a continuous circulation of members among them. In a single colony of the Society of Brothers, for example, fully one-third of the adult population in 1956 were former members of numerous other utopian groups, including Banner.[14] Similarly, six of the twenty-nine adult residents in Banner are utopian "repeaters," having lived in two or more such communities before this one. As one of them remarked, "Why, Fred and I haven't lived in a normal, ordinary community in sixteen years of marriage." They have threaded their lives through a series of utopias, shifting from one to another as disillusionment deepens, or as groups disband or become swallowed into one another.

These circumstances obtained to some extent even among the utopians of nineteenth-century America, in spite of the relatively inefficient communications and transportation technology of that time: "The returners, who had left dissatisfied but came back

[14] David Stanley Tillson, *A Pacifist Community in Peacetime: An Introductory Description of the Woodcrest Bruderhof at Rifton, New York* (Unpublished dissertation, Syracuse University, 1958), pp. 47–52.

after a while in the cold world, the repeaters, who tried different varieties of community and were ever ready to join a new experiment, and the excommunitarians in the native radical movement, all testify to the permanent orientation acquired or confirmed in the communities."[15]

Students at the school, participants in the children's and family camps, and many of the customers of the pharmaceutical business and printing shop are friends or acquaintances of community residents. Formal recruitment of students through advertisements in radical magazines and brochures mailed to large numbers of potential supporters brings in an insignificant proportion of the student body each year. By the same token, the proportion of customers attracted by formal advertising is small. The exception here, of course, is the locally oriented used clothing store.

Beyond the importance of Banner's network relationships for recruitment and economic purposes, however, there is another aspect to them which seems more noteworthy for the continuation of the community organization. It is related to the very purpose for which Banner was created: that of making an alternative social order as an example to a diseased world. The utopians are aware that Banner community is not widely known. They tend to equate isolation with selfishness and escapism, and they regard both attributes as immoral. Involvement in the great issues of our age, they say, is a moral duty of every man. At the same time, some residents do see themselves as enjoying in Banner a rest—perhaps permanent, perhaps only temporary—from the immense pressures for conformity and compromise in American life. Yet closing themselves off from the problems of the world outside, in their own view, would be tantamount to admitting that their motives are only self-indulgent hopes of personal

[15] T. D. Seymour Bassett, "The Secular Utopian Socialists," in D. D. Egbert and Stow Persons, eds., *Socialism and American Life* (Princeton, N.J.: Princeton University Press, 1952), Vol. 1, p. 203.

improvement. As the community's "hope for success in history" —to borrow a phrase from Bassett—has dimmed since 1946, doubts have increased among the residents about their motivations for remaining. "If we are not here to light a beacon for mankind, then why continue?" they seem to ask themselves. Their guilt is not satisfactorily assuaged by opinions even as adulatory as that in a Quaker visitor's letter in 1959: "I think that the Banner community is world-shaking. In [George] Fox's day, one dedicated Friend could shake the land for 20 miles around. But in this day of rapid communication, a community like that at Banner can shake the whole world . . . at least give it a tremor. Louise and I had a renewing experience at Banner." "Utopian" itself connotes a visionary dream of retreating from the harsh world of reality, and they resist this particular label for their endeavor.

Participation in radical reformist activity outside the confines of the community has taken on new significance in furnishing a means by which the utopians can express their dissatisfaction with existing social institutions and work for change. An uneasy peace prevails between them and the local Appalachian people. If they were to stage demonstrations in the local towns, the sullen disapproval of locals might break out in open hostility and violence. The usual technique for celebrating important occasions, like Hiroshima Day (August 10), is to send a delegation from Banner to ceremonies held in urban centers. This appears to be a somewhat acceptable substitute for arranging local affairs. Besides the danger of provoking a hostile response from local people, the utopians see little to be gained by such display: no one would notice anyhow, they contend.

Maintenance of personal relationships with individuals outside the community permits the residents to dramatize their efforts and transform them from the ineffectual acts of a small band of dissidents into potentially momentous innovations in social education. Much of the communication between residents and their allies takes the form of reaffirmation of verbal symbols: non-violence, community, personal responsibility, world brother-hood, cooperation, and so on. Only on specific occasions and for special purposes do they assemble with their allies for coordinated social activity. Whenever they try to explore the meaning of these symbols, it often becomes evident that the presumed agreement does not exist. A visiting Catholic priest, for instance, was thought to share the Quaker residents' view of pacifism. In discussing with him the Vietnam war, however, it soon developed that he believed in the concept of "just war." It was only this particular war, an unjust one in his opinion, which he opposed. As one of the Quakers said later, "He just holds material values above human values, that's all—he's for war to defend property rights."

V I

Utopian visions are delicate constructions. Faith in the possibility of wholesale social change through non-violent means is difficult to maintain in the face of persistent evidence to the contrary. Given their shaky ideological foundations, it is no surprise that individual utopian communities rarely endure for very long. This is particularily so for secular ones, where the program is more one of experimentation with new social forms than precise adherence to divinely sanctioned ones. As the Society of Brothers, a Christian group, has stated its idea of communal living: "The call to community is no call to an experiment. We dare not experiment with community life."[16] The usual route for secular

---

[16] Society of Brothers, *Ten Years of Communal Living: The Wheathill Bruderhof, 1942–1952* (Bromdon, England: Plough Publishing Co., 1952), p. 40.

utopias, and many times for religious ones as well, is a gradual surrender to conventionality. The choice seems to lie between compromising adjustment to non-utopian institutions, or extinction.

But by committing their efforts to purposes beyond those of a small community, Banner's utopians need not despair when they see, as they surely have, that the community is destined to remain unimitated on a large scale. Hedging their reformist bets, so to speak, and spreading their effort in several directions, they can count on some success, however small, at the same time that they prepare themselves for a measure of failure. In the battle for racial equality, for example, their contribution can be seen as helping to bring about a number of desirable changes. Their equally ardent fight for a cooperative and peaceful social order has, so far, been inconclusive. Nevertheless, they take as an encouraging development the recent increase in pacifist publicity and activity.

While the implication of this utopian community in a network of allies somewhat dilutes the utopian vision, particularly that aspect which aims for the creation of new social worlds, it is also a kind of ideological insurance. By settling for a variety of small gains, they avoid the disaster of a single great failure. Having admitted to themselves that Banner community wields little influence, they still are not forced to see their continued residence in this isolated locale as selfish and escapist. In this way, their outside involvements provide one means of alleviating the burden of escapism.